From

MOTHER AND DAUGHTER

to

FRIENDS

NANCY ANISTON

A Memoir

From

MOTHER AND DAUGHTER

to

FRIENDS

Prometheus Books

59 John Glenn Drive
Amherst, New York 14228-2197

Published 1999 by Prometheus Books

Inquiries should be addressed to
Prometheus Books, 59 John Glenn Drive, Amherst, New York 14228–2197.
VOICE: 716–691–0133, ext. 207. FAX: 716–564–2711.
WWW.PROMETHEUSBOOKS.COM

03 02 01 00 99   5 4 3 2 1

Library of Congress Cataloging-in-Publication Data

Aniston, Nancy.
     From mother and daughter to friends / Nancy Aniston.
         p.   cm.
     ISBN 1-57392-772-4 (alk. paper)
     1. Aniston, Jennifer. 2. Aniston, Nancy. I. Title.
PN2287.A62A3   1999
791.45'028'092—dc21
[B]   99-42416
                                                                              CIP

Printed in the United States of America on acid-free paper

To my beloved children, John Melick and Jennifer Aniston, with love and gratitude for the gift of motherhood. To Joan, Jean, Linda, and Sally for the gift of sisterhood.

CONTENTS

Penelope Savalas Boardman
FOREWORD

NANCY HAS ALWAYS BEEN A part of my life. Ours is a friendship I dearly cherish. I have heard fragments of her story over the years but never the whole. I am extremely proud of Nancy for finding her own voice and not writing as someone's daughter, wife, ex-wife, or mother. This book compiles Nancy's reminiscences and reflections expressed from her unique perspective. That may not seem terribly monumental to my generation of women, but it is.

I am considered by those who apply these kinds of categories as a member of Generation X. While I do not place a lot of value on labels, certain generalizations are true; women of my generation tend to take for granted the great strides that our predecessors, Baby Boomer women, made toward advancing women's opportunities. The choices available to us were unimaginable to

Nancy and my own mother. They followed the rules and did what their fathers and husbands expected of them. Nancy and my mother each became divorce statistics in the 1970s. By then feminism was radicalized, and no matter what each felt about the inequities of their lot, they still had children to raise, feed, and educate. They were not emotionally disposed to joining the cause, or raised to necessarily think *for* themselves or *of* themselves.

By telling her story, Nancy has come to express her point of view with characteristic sensitivity to others. Her thoughtful explanation of events, and of her feelings and actions, have helped me to come to an understanding of my own mother. This journal of family history will undoubtedly assure appreciation of Nancy by her little grandchild.

PREFACE

THE OFTEN DEBATED VIEW THAT it's better to parent like a friend began to take hold in our culture when I was raising my two children, Johnny and Jennifer. I didn't subscribe to this view because I believed that dependent children need "parents" to guide them. At seventeen my son left home to attend college in another state and the tendency to nurture him weaned quite naturally. With my daughter it was entirely different.

A few months after Johnny moved away my husband and I divorced. Jen was only nine years old when half of our family left home and as often happens with a single parent, an especially close bond was forged between us. But by the time she was in her mid-twenties differences in our thinking led to estrangement. I was devastated. I began to write a journal of happy memories to help manage the pain, and in the process I came to realize that our

11

"close" relationship was actually codependent and needed to change. I discovered that the roles of both mother and daughter must give way to a more mutually understanding, nonjudgmental, and respectful relationship that is more akin to what often takes place between good friends.

In recent years life experiences, both our own and those of others, have tended to replace social mores and dictates as the way many people formulate their philosophical approach to life's challenges. I believe that this tendency is evident in the abundance of support groups and self-improvement books that help us to think our way through emotional pain. I've written my story in the fervent hope of making a similar contribution.

Author's note: Some names have been changed to protect the privacy of certain individuals.

ACKNOWLEDG-MENTS

I WISH TO EXPRESS my gratitude to Coral Leigh, a friend who, from the beginning, understood and believed in the need for women to tell their stories. Her encouragement helped launch this project and was the force that carried me forward, many times, when I wanted to give up. I'm also grateful to Mala Powers, Diane Davenport, Leigh Lombardi, Penelope Savalas Boardman, and Bari Borsky who so generously gave of their time to read and reread my manuscript, offering suggestions while lavishing help and unwavering support. My gratitude goes to those friends who, through the years, witnessed the twists and turns of my destiny, for taking the time to carefully read through the text for objectivity and/or accuracy, and for their well-timed words of support—in addition to those mentioned above: John and Susan Dooley, Reverend Jim Hindes, Lynn Savalas, Lee and Penny

13

Thompson, Jack Thomas, and Patti Secrease. To my big sisters Joan and Jean who parented me when I was little and at times when I wasn't, thank you for your enthusiasm and pep talks to "get *it* out there." My deepest gratitude is reserved for Molly Reynolds for the light of her love that shines then and now. And finally to Steven L. Mitchell, my editor at Prometheus Books, who guided me through the very complicated process of publishing with patience, understanding, humor, honesty, and an admirable sense of fairness.

Chapter 1
"DON'T WORRY, I KNOW IT'S YOUR FIRST INTERVIEW. . . ."

I T WAS FEBRUARY 1996, AND I still felt the glow from a glorious Christmas with my two children. I had no idea that the rogue tabloid media was about to attack my family.

Unsuspecting, I entered a room at the luxurious Peninsula Hotel in Beverly Hills to tape my first televised interview. Through an agreement I had made with the producers of the show, the interview was to be restricted to the Waldorf method of teaching—it was not to be about my celebrity daughter!

As I checked my hair and makeup in a lavish powder room of marble and mirrored walls, I felt a bit uneasy. I wanted to tell Jen that I had been given this chance to inform people about her old school, but I wasn't able to reach her. My friend Dodi had suggested that she come with me; I felt a surge of gratitude as I found myself comforted by her effusive support.

"Ms. Aniston, we're almost ready."

I climbed over lighting equipment and slipped into the chair facing a young woman who responded to the concern on my face. "Don't worry, I know it's your first interview. I will keep our promise and limit my questions to your topic."

The room flooded with light, and my heart pounded as I held both hands to still the shaking. Would I know the answer to all of her questions? Was I well enough prepared? My mouth went dry. "Yes," I told them, "I'm ready." More shaking. Calm down, Nancy, I told myself, it'll soon be over. I was surprised to be that nervous.

When the interviewer asked if there was anything else I wanted to say about the school, I knew it was almost over. There followed a few casual comments about Jennifer's hair, how I felt about her success on *Friends*, and when they said, "Let's wrap," everyone seemed happy, especially me. I managed to take hold of my nerves and for more than an hour of intelligent, well-formed questions about the school, I had given some pretty insightful answers.

On the drive home I asked Dodi again and again, "Are you sure it was good?" She generously repeated, as many times as I asked, "Are you kidding? It was great!" Dodi then added that she could never be so articulate in front of a camera, and considering it was my first televised interview she was impressed.

I still worried. "But will Jen be impressed?"

"Why shouldn't she be? Of course she'll be. Not everyone gets a chance to plug something they care about on prime-time TV."

"Their offer to plug the school was tempting. But it doesn't make sense that they would be that anxious just to get the first interview with me. I can't shake this uneasy feeling. I should have followed my instinct to decline."

Dodi became a little impatient. "You know that people have always loved to see the parents of celebrities and I heard the producer tell you that their audience would be very interested in hearing about the school."

I began to feel better. Yes, I had furthered a cause I believed in since the late sixties. Now more parents would know about a teaching system that is a positive force in our crumbling society. I hoped I had made it clear that Waldorf graduates are often productive, well-balanced young people, who can make positive contributions—important factors for the future of our country.

"You should feel good about yourself," Dodi said.

"I do. So, thanks for talking me into doing it, Dodi."

"And you'll thank me again in four days when it airs."

The four days dragged by. Jen still hadn't returned my calls. I wanted to tell Jen to watch the show but her hectic schedule made reaching her next to impossible. I told myself it really didn't matter because by now interviews are not a big deal to her. It was enough to know that my sisters and a few friends would be watching. I was nervous and excited.

When the show aired and my segment ended I couldn't believe what I had seen. They had deleted the entire portion about the school! All that aired were those few innocuous comments about Jennifer, spliced intermittently with some clips from a rather silly videotape of Jen and some friends from high school behaving like typical teenagers—a tape I didn't even know existed! There were more empty comments from me about a mother's pride and more silly tape. Not one mention of the school! My sole purpose for doing the interview had been deleted. I sat there stunned. I felt stupidly naive. I was livid! Clearly I'd been deceived in order to get an interview about Jen.

Dodi called and said, "See? Weren't you terrific?"

"No! There wasn't one word about the school! Don't you see they tricked me? And that friendly young woman even hugged me good-bye. How embarrassing."

"Why? You were charming and I must say, you looked great."

"Don't you see what they've done?"

"But people love to see celebrities' mothers. You just made a few nice comments about your daughter. What's wrong with that? I know you'll feel better tomorrow."

Dodi didn't understand why I was so upset. And my sister Joan failed to see the problem when she called a few hours later. But I couldn't forget the betrayal. I went to bed early, wanting to disappear into sleep. Pulling the pillow over my head, I hoped Jen hadn't seen it.

After tossing and turning for more than an hour, I flew out of bed when the telephone rang. It was Jen, but her voice was so distorted by rage I didn't recognize it at first. Stunned by her angry words and accusations, I hardly spoke. Then I just stood there, reeling from her abrupt hang-up. Jen was very angry that I had appeared on the show and said she would never forgive me! Despite the deals I'd made with God the one thing I feared had happened. I'd lost my daughter. In an instant my life was reduced to irrelevance.

I wandered through the dark searching for a concept, a thought, anything to hang onto. What was so terrible about being on *that* show? Did Jen actually believe that I would knowingly hurt her? Did she honestly think I would risk alienating the one person who had been the focus of my deepest concern for more than twenty-six years? It was tearing me apart that Jennifer, of all people, didn't realize that it was *I* who had been betrayed.

In the long night that followed I moved from room to room, dazed by those terrible words, "I'll never forgive you!" NEVER echoed loud in my head. Dropping the heavy load of disbelief into a chair, I wondered what had happened to the trust we had built through years of pulling together to bear a reality neither of us wanted.

How long might NEVER be? The prospect of my daughter in that black hole of estrangement filled the night with ghosts from the past. Hadn't it been me she'd always depended on? In its second year now, with the popularity of *Friends* catapulting her to fame, phone calls became more scarce, but I was always there if she needed help or when bouts of anxiety proved overwhelming. With agents, managers, lawyers, publicists, business managers, and even a few friends all vying for a piece of her success, who would protect her? With me gone anyone or anything could slip into that void.

The thought of being shut out now with that wall of people forming around her chilled me to the bone. Would hangers-on, motivated by self-interest, gain from our separation? Were they encouraging her to become distanced from me?

More pacing. I found myself remembering Jen as a newborn baby and her occasional bouts of crying that no one could calm but me. I sat in the misery of that night, picturing my baby's grin breaking through her sobs as I patted the shrieking bundle until calm and confidence returned. For a moment I forgot the sharp sound of her words as my heart warmed with remembered joy. In a Kafkaesque moment I felt joy and pain at the same time.

But soon, recalling the fear she experienced as a child only added to my concern. It stirred a protective tendency that had grown even stronger during my years of single parenting. How would I bear this loss? How could I stand never knowing if she's safe or well? Never. NEVER?

It was impossible to accept that a misunderstanding over something so innocent, so well-intended, caused this life-altering reaction. It simply couldn't be that Jen had misinterpreted my motives as something so terrible that I was never to be forgiven. NEVER!

It went on like that throughout the long sleepless night. The severity of those words simply wouldn't sink into my brain. My daughter's implied lack of trust reduced my reasoning to shards of doubt. Had something else come between us without my knowledge? It's true, I had been grumbling about how she was allowing too many people to make important decisions, and we were bickering at times. But isn't it a mother's job to caution against parasites who might feed on her child's success?

"Mom, you don't trust anyone!"

And wasn't I right to say it was foolish to hire a manager after the efforts of a wonderful agent had already garnered success and fame? Why would she simply hand over another percentage?

"Mom, it's the nineties; things have changed since you were in the business."

Okay. I backed off. Or did I? Spasms of self-doubt and self-loathing were gnawing at my faith in the past. Had she seen through my efforts and felt uncomfortable? Or had I lost her long before this deceptive interview?

That question hit with such a force that my breathing seemed to stop. I was shivering with cold as the first faint light of morning peeked through the kitchen window. When had I ceased to be a safe place, the one she could count on? Or was that just another incorrect assumption an my part?

My imagination was running wild. I reached for the coffee tin, placed grounds in the pot, and watched the dark liquid run out. The muscles in my face hurt from crying. Pull yourself together, Nancy, I thought to myself, you'll sort it out. It will make sense. Hasn't everything always worked out for the best?

As the sun came up my terrifying thoughts began to fade in the light. Look, hadn't Jenny once told me that I was the only person she knew who would always tell her the truth? Of course. She'll phone and say she overreacted. We'll talk it over and this nightmare will end.

I buried my burning face in cold water. The telephone rang and my heart nearly stopped. Please be Jen. I grabbed for the receiver and though it turned out to be one of her friends, I welcomed it as a chance to have someone intercede with my true intentions. But I soon realized that the caller just wanted to restate hurtful accusations as he insisted that I should have known better than to appear on a tabloid TV show. I'm embarrassed every time I remember my futile attempts to explain that I was merely trying to plug a good cause, and that I had been betrayed. But the caller repeatedly twisted my meaning and my efforts were wasted on ears that only listened for a word that would yield some preconceived advantage. My plea for understanding had gone on too long and when the phone abruptly went dead I was devastated.

I knew on some level that I had lost Jen forever. If a friend of hers was allowed to speak to me that way, something was terribly wrong. I sat on the kitchen stool trying to hold myself together. What began with her birth and had grown strong through the years was gone. "Thrice I trembled to the depths of my being."

Demeter's words upon discovering that her beloved daughter Persephone was lost to a distant world could not convey more pain than what I was feeling. My daughter, like Demeter's, was lost to a world where I didn't belong.

I'm not sure exactly how many days passed before I called my son, Johnny, for support or possibly to ask him to intervene on my behalf. I wasn't sure what. I knew how much he loved us both and when he didn't return my call, I respected his silence as a wish to stay neutral. Johnny had married his lovely Shannon the previous summer, and with a baby on the way, I refused to let my problems detract from their joy. I decided to wait for him to call me. But the one loss I had prayed to be spared could not be borne alone. I turned for help to a few dedicated, carefully chosen friends, and I also found that weekly counseling sessions at church strengthened the glue that held my shattered life together.

I had been seeing a doctor who specializes in Chinese herbs and often imparts great truths and words of wisdom to his patients. Sometimes we just talked and his understanding lent added support. He explained that in Buddhism they say that our children are the source of life's greatest joy as well as its greatest pain. That's true, I thought, my children have been a source of infinite joy and there was no denying that the threat of losing Jennifer was causing the worst pain I'd ever known. Doctor Kang softly explained that my child had left the nest and I must let her go.

As a young woman I had read a wise man's words about children: "For their souls dwell in the house of tomorrow, which you cannot visit, not even in your dreams." The wisdom of Kahlil Gibran was more appealing to me as a romantic twenty-year-old than now, when its true meaning was threatening a reality too terrible to imagine.

How could I let go when I believed deep inside that she still needed me and still depended on me to be there? I thought of the time, shortly after her birth, when the first signs of fear surfaced. Two friends had come by to pay a call on me and my husband, John, and to meet our new baby girl. Jen surprised us all by greeting their unfamiliar faces with an outburst of hysterical crying. Our peaceful baby wailed on and on until it became obvious that if I was ever to calm her down, I must do it alone in the quiet of my bedroom. We soon discovered that those two friends were not going to be the only people to receive such a greeting. Even her daddy encountered a few. We never knew when to expect another outburst. With certain people our baby girl seemed to experience something quite terrifying.

She clung to me through many such episodes. To ease her anxiety, it took my repeated assurances that people are kind and there was nothing to fear. At last, one day, our three-year-old announced, "Mommy, my favorite word is *they're here.*" It was a definite sign of change and a relief to everyone that Jenny's natural love of people had triumphed over mistrust. But a kind of reticence, bordering on fear, remained. Who would understand that now?

Each day began and ended with the hope that Jen would call. Maybe one of her friends would remind her of my unconditional love. It felt strange that the call didn't come, yet somehow the hope that it would helped me make it through a most difficult period in my life.

I was grateful for the help of my friends. The few innocuous comments they had viewed on a tape of the tabloid TV show led to the consensus that Jen's reaction must be rooted in something that happened long ago. My friend Bari urged me to give Jen the space she was seeking. Bari, a classic beauty in her late forties, whose grace radiates from years of spiritual study, offered fruits of wisdom from her own passage into womanhood. When she spoke of her deceased mother, a deep sadness confirmed the depth of understanding she brought to me. Her voice was tender and full of regret as she expressed how she felt misunderstood as a daughter. In a most gentle way she said that if I were ever going to have a good relationship with Jennifer, this separation was necessary. Bari cautioned that it might take a long time to discover the real cause of Jen's anger and promised to be there for support if I needed to talk. She urged me to call anytime, day or night. In the few short years since we met, I had found Bari to be a wise and devoted friend. I knew she was right; it would take time to discover what had pushed Jenny away. Until then, my first job was to learn how to live without her.

I managed to turn away from the pain and my journey began. I soon discovered that many women suffered from estranged relationships with their grown daughters. Each one was unique but all alike in that they involved misunderstanding, anger, broken bonds, and almost unspeakable pain. The media is saturated with examples of families breaking ties. Like a magnet, similar situations were drawn to my attention, bringing to the surface a host of issues. Surely those women loved their daughters as much as I loved mine. No doubt they tried as hard as I did to be the mother each of us felt we never had. Yet there they were, for millions of people to witness, several successful young actresses admitting to Barbara Walters that they had ended all contact with their mothers. Why? Were these mothers as devastated or as shocked as I? As bewildered and confused? What do they think about during sleepless nights? What magic helps them cope with the loneliness or bear the reality of this drastic change in our cultural view, almost unheard of a generation ago?

In earlier times, to describe a truly despicable person one said, "He'd cheat his own mother." This reflected a regard for one's mother that only the worst scoundrel would violate. It was becoming apparent to me that there's been a shift in our thinking when celebrities, admired by so many, express this contrasting change in values as acceptable. What has brought about this unfortunate change? Had society's distorted view influenced Jen?

I began feeling helpless, my motives misunderstood. As the weeks passed, one moment I felt defensive, while the next was filled with doubt. Had I failed to give Jen what she needed when divorce forced me to raise her alone? Most women feel a natural protection for their children, and mine strengthened as I watched my nine-year-old daughter, tormented by the abrupt and unexpected departure of her dad, just a few months after her big brother had left home for college. I wanted to fill the void but two empty chairs at our dinner table were a daily reminder that half of our family was gone. All I could do was watch helplessly as sadness invaded Jen, and I simply surrounded her with my love. I took her everywhere with me and in no time we became adoring buddies.

Wasn't it only natural that, given those circumstances, we developed a closer relationship than would ordinarily have occurred? A mother-daughter dependency was inevitable and we enjoyed it until Jen's early teens found her rebelling. I gave her more freedom but, as with all normal teenagers, Jen wanted too much and my efforts to counter the rebellion created resentment. I was sure we had made it through those difficult years and had moved on. Was I wrong? Was something unresolved from that period contributing to our current situation?

There were more questions than answers. Had I completely failed as a mother, the job to which I had devoted most of my adult life? Why was I feeling this terrible shame? What causes a mother's good intentions to be misinterpreted? How had I lost Jen's trust?

Questions fueled my determination to find answers. I vowed to work with this cruel stroke of destiny rather than against it, and in the process I might also discover what lurked behind society's negative view of the maternal role.

A comforting concept that I had read many times in books of Rudolf Steiner ran through my mind: "A painful blow of fate can bring inner growth, wisdom, renewed strength, and a heightened ability to love." Perhaps the loss I'd regarded as too much to bear was necessary. I vowed to find a way to accept what was happening and in the process to discover what it was I needed to learn.

Chapter 2
SWITCHING FOCUS

I HAD LOST CONTACT WITH Jen in early February and it was already April. My resolve to find answers was going nowhere fast. With no word from my kids I was losing ground. If I had gained strength or wisdom from surviving hardship in the past, there wasn't much to call upon now. Each day I sank deeper into depression.

I had always believed in a better tomorrow but I couldn't imagine a future without my daughter. A good sense of humor had helped me through many hard times but there was little to laugh about now. Life's challenges had always been like climbing mountains that offered a view not seen before, but I doubted that my legs were capable of scaling what seemed to be the highest mountain of all. Johnny and Jennifer were the core of my life and it was hard to live with the fact that I had failed one of them. I felt that years of effort were worth less than nothing. My minister, a family counselor for more than twenty years, said that all children need to break free from their parents and this was merely Jennifer's way. There was the hint of a suggestion that I needed to break free, too. He added that I was being too hard on myself, and that I must find a way to pull out of this hole.

After endless weeks of swimming in self-pity, I knew I had to do something. My whole life needed reevaluating and I had to find a way to switch focus. Perhaps by retracing the path that led to the spot I was in, I'd find a way out. But in order to embark on a thorough review of the past, I'd have to remember what had been long forgotten. Could I go through all that?

In the midst of my musing the telephone rang. When it turned out to be Jennifer's secretary my heart nearly stopped. But that sinking feeling returned when the subject was just business. As if nothing had changed, she casually said that they urgently needed to find some documents for Jen or there would be serious tax problems. Since I didn't have the documents, she asked if I might try to locate them.

I contacted a woman at our bank who had always been friendly and she agreed to help. It was no easy task and there were weeks of phone calls before our efforts succeeded in obtaining photocopies of the much-needed records. Because it was tax time everything was much more difficult and I was impressed by her willingness to work so hard. She said she was just doing her job.

When Jen's secretary came to pick up the papers she mentioned that everyone, especially the business manager, was grateful, and yes, the woman at the bank would be sent flowers. Hungry for word, I asked how Jenny was feeling and what she was doing. It was a blow to hear the secretary reply, "I don't want to get in the middle."

"What middle? I'm her mother. Please understand, I need to know."

But she repeated the middle thing, gave me a half-hug, then kissed the air next to my cheek, grabbed the large packet of documents, and left.

I had been demoted to stranger by a woman who behaved as if my own daughter needed to be protected from me. Nevertheless it was a source of pride knowing that we had accomplished what Jennifer's well-paid help couldn't. But the message was pretty clear: I would have to find a way to live with this paralyzing sadness.

Birds singing near the window reminded me that spring, my favorite time of year, had finally arrived. Yet grief persisted. I was missing Jen, and weeks of heavy rain in sunny California only added to my somber mood. I was engulfed by a loneliness that was reminiscent of the feeling I had when Jen first left home. In 1987, Jen finished high school, and less than two years later she decided that building a career would be easier in California. She left our New York apartment to stay with her father while looking for a place of her own. My home felt brutally empty. The good news was that five years after our 1980 divorce, John had moved back to Los Angeles and would be there for her. I was now feeling the same loneliness as on the day she left. Gloom continued to fall with the rain until a random thought lifted my spirits. It would soon be Mother's Day, a holiday Jennifer always loved to celebrate. As a child she drew wonderful handmade cards declaring her love and later on, spent hours browsing specialty stores to find just the right verse. I pictured the delight on her face when she saw how deeply I'd been touched. This memory brought a pleasant and unexpected wash of joy.

I tenaciously held onto that joy by returning my thoughts to my favorite Mother's Day, made possible only by Jennifer's move to California.

I was still living in our apartment in Manhattan, and one day Jen phoned to say that a special-delivery package would arrive and I *must* be home to accept it. The urgency in her voice made me suspect that since it was Mother's Day on Sunday, it could be flowers that might wilt if I wasn't there to receive them. With great anticipation I waited. In the afternoon my intercom rang to announce a delivery. I buzzed to open the lobby door. In the time it takes to ride the elevator to our high-rise apartment, a knock came and a muffled voice from out in the hall said, "Special delivery." I opened the door and shrieked to find Jennifer standing there, suitcase in hand, with a big grin announcing, "Happy Mother's Day, Mom!" After hugs, kisses, and happy tears, she told me that she was mine for the whole weekend and wouldn't see anyone else. We spent the entire three days together and it was one of the most wonderful times we've ever shared.

That glorious memory filled my heart, lifted my mood, and brought renewed hope!

Yes, I thought, in spite of our misunderstanding, I'll hear from Jen on Mother's Day. It's only a few weeks away and there will be a card, flowers, and some contact. That's all it will take. No need for an apology. The contact will be enough to express her wish to go on with our normal life. No more separation. No more anger. In our usual mother/daughter squabbles we would often move past anger without apologies. Trust, love, and mutual understanding had always been enough. I was definitely feeling better.

Mother's Day came and went without a word. Darkness once again overtook my mood. It was one bumpy ride.

I had heard about daily journals being an effective tool in

emotional healing and how the process seemed to be helping many people. It was reported that making a log of the past somehow brought insights that helped heal deep emotional pain. Recalling Jen's fear as a child, my overprotective response already seemed to contain the hint of a helpful revelation. Maybe if I were to write down sad memories as well as happy ones, I might find what I was looking for. Several years ago I had attempted to write an autobiography but felt I was too young. It was definitely time to give it another try.

Day after day I returned to the word processor and dug deeper into the past—our past. A wealth of memories appeared. There were smiles, laughter, tears, and insights that offered more than I'd ever expected. The activity itself was lifting me out of the "hole," and for the first time in several months I was moving in a direction of my own choosing.

I began getting my feet wet by dipping them in the stream that belonged to my parents and my first experience with loss. . . .

Like most parents, mine had good intentions that were warped by demons from their youth. The story begins with my paternal grandparents, Francis Dow and Ellen Mclean, who emigrated from Scotland and settled in the coldest part of Maine. They gave birth to my father, Gordon Dow. Grandfather was a direct descendant of the Stuarts, which made Mary, Queen of Scots, our relative. A fierce, cranky man known as a strict disciplinarian, Grandfather Dow insisted that his children be well educated, have impeccable manners, and be gracious to everyone. Gordon grew up to be a charming man who possessed all of those qualities, but there was also a side full of rage. Gordon was only four years old in 1911 when his mother, Ellen, died. He told of climbing onto

31

her bed and hugging her dead body as he pleaded, "Mommy, talk to me." It was inevitable that the brutality of the life that followed created a lot of anger in that little boy. There were stories of a nameless stepmother who treated him badly and, no doubt, fueled the fire within. The handsome young man who met and married my mother, Louise Grieco, must have been sitting on an emotional powder keg.

Both of my parents came from good families but, like many New Englanders at that time, they had limited access to their feelings, especially when it came to showing affection. My maternal grandfather, Louis Grieco, was a hardworking Italian immigrant who came from Melitto, Italy, around the turn of the century. He soon landed a job as the private barber to John D. Rockefeller himself, no less, but left his employ to become a successful business man on Fisher's Island in New York.

Grandfather Grieco wanted to be affectionate with his family but was inhibited by Grandmother Grieco, who only expressed feelings through dissatisfaction. Their one daughter, Louise, impressed everyone with her brilliant mind. A private school in New London, Connecticut, awarded her a tuition-free scholarship for high school because she was such a good student. Grandfather didn't like the idea of gratis tuition. He said they didn't need charity.

The roar of the twenties was abruptly stilled in 1929 by the stock-market crash and the thirties became a decade of misery for America. In the midst of what came to be known as the Great Depression, Gordon and Louise decided to marry. Millions of people were out of work. In no time Mother was pregnant and surprised everyone when twins, Jean and Joan, were born. Two years later I arrived, but Father couldn't find work to provide for our growing family. At times we had to live with my maternal grandparents in the big house where Mother was raised. After the birth of a fourth child, Linda, we moved to government housing in New Britain, Connecticut. World War II had lifted the country out of its financial crisis. The war had created jobs for everyone, including my parents. Both found factory work. Mother worked a night shift that overlapped Father's day shift for a few hours in the evening. No older than seven, my oldest sister, Joan, was expected to take care of us. Four little girls did a pretty good job staying safe with no adult in the house. We knew that when the air-raid siren howled it was important to either pull down the black shades or turn off all the lights. I was scared that bombs might fall any minute. We sometimes complained that Joan bossed us around, but mostly we had fun playing forbidden games like sliding down the stairs with our raincoats.

Three years after Linda, a fifth child, Little Martha, arrived; she was born with what we now call Down's syndrome. Joan learned quickly how to make formula and to feed her a bottle and never once complained about changing diapers. When my last sister, Sally, was born, Mother had to stop working and our family knew the kind of poverty that often sent us to bed hungry. Severe poverty beset us once again. Father had the idea that life in California might be easier so one day we all squeezed into the car and he drove our family west. We settled in North Hollywood, a lovely, peaceful section of the San Fernando Valley. Shortly after our arrival in 1945, the end of the war was announced by a loud roar over our house. Nearby, the well-camouflaged Lockheed aircraft plant sent a squadron of P-38s to buzz the city and the noise sent me running outside. I squealed with delight as the sky filled with hundreds of colorful party balloons and neighbors ran out into the street. Everyone was happy and I knew we wouldn't have to worry that bombs might fall anymore.

Universal Pictures studio was near our house and Father was hired as a security guard at the front gate. I often wondered if he had a secret wish to be an actor and was quietly building a dream. But with six children to feed, Father couldn't afford to dream. Wages were pitifully low in those days, and with six children he was forced to take a second job. But there never seemed to be enough to cover all of our needs. He soon became overtired and easily exploded with anger. People from work or neighbors who knew about our family sent parcels of discarded clothing. It was exciting to rummage through those items to find something that fit, but very disappointing when nothing did.

There wasn't much laughter in our home, but I found great joy in playing with Little Martha. She didn't learn to walk until age three, and although she couldn't really talk, something about her made me feel happy. She had a sweet smile and she liked to be held. She was often sick but never complained, and that touched my heart more than anything. When she was four years old, a bad cough sent her to the hospital, and I knew real terror. I heaved a sigh of relief when they brought her home, even though she had a big scar and one lung was gone. It was cold in the back bedroom that we shared with Linda and I tried to make sure the little sister I adored stayed warm. I would brush the tangles from her hair and one day she surprised everyone by saying "pretty" because no one thought to teach her any words. Father said she couldn't learn.

One day after school Jean, the younger twin, ran down to the sidewalk with a strange look on her face and said, "Guess what? Martha died while we were in school today." Died? I knew she had a bad cold but no one said anything about dying! I ran and hid in the garage because in our family crying was viewed as stupid or bad. I was in there a long time, hugging my knees. When I was called to come in the house, I felt a warm trickle of urine run down my legs.

Mother said we had to go to church and give Little Martha to God. Father told us to be quiet and not to giggle or act silly. We sat in a row on folding chairs in our freshly ironed dresses and no one thought to giggle. I gazed, without moving, into that bed of white satin where my little sister lay. She looked healthy to me and very much alive in a soft pink dress, the only one she'd ever had, and a small bouquet of pink rosebuds in her hands. It appeared as if she were sleeping. Little Martha, get up, let's go home. When they lowered the top, I didn't care what anyone said; I couldn't stop crying. At home everything was different. Nothing ever felt the same again.

My parents said death was a blessing for Little Martha. But we'd left her alone in a box and I couldn't see how that was a blessing. I would lie on the floor of the linen closet and bury my head in a stack of her folded clothes and cry, "Please, God, let her come home." I promised to try harder to keep her warm and to even give her my share of ice cream. When it looked like He wouldn't be sending her back, I told God that she liked to have her hair brushed and to please make a fuss when she says "pretty."

The last time I went to that closet, all of the clothes with the scent of Little Martha were gone.

The harshness of our life created an atmosphere of tense fighting and bickering. There were just too many kids vying for attention from parents who were too stressed, tired, and damaged by their own upbringing to offer affection. My sisters and I

35

fought fiercely for the scraps of love that fell from a nearly empty table. But we also had fun.

As grown women we often reminisced about the four army cots that lined the small, otherwise bare room where we older girls slept. We laughed to recall how being so close in age (all four of us were born within four years) and all attending grammar school made it hard to fall asleep at bedtime. There was so much to giggle about. When our whispers got too loud, Mother stormed in wielding a hairbrush to firmly swat our behinds, one after the other. She'd leave with a stern warning and close the door. We'd giggle even louder and she'd return immediately, only this time the hairbrush landed harder and sleep was more appealing. Four little girls, with sorely stinging bottoms, didn't make another sound. Not that night. We remembered that it never stopped us from misbehaving again. We had each other.

Recalling the loss of Little Martha brought a torrent of tears that joined with the present sadness of recognizing how I might have failed my own kids. I wondered if every kid feels that childhood is tough. During a brief walk a joke came to mind: "It might be easier to be a kid if you weren't so young." It didn't help. I returned to resurrect a happy memory.

I tried to recall the special joy a parent experiences when thinking about their children. But when I sat down to begin typing, a stream of random impressions overtook my brain. My head filled with accusations, slights, and rude behavior from the growing number of people in Jen's world, a world I understood less and less. I started wondering if the door to her world, once such a familiar place, had been closing to me for some time.

It was hard to get started but I refused to give up. I just sat there, staring at the word processor, with little access to controlled thought. Then suddenly, after what seemed to be hours, as if by magic the mental chaos cleared. Lovely details started to surface and I was finally able to rest my attention on a most glorious moment in time.

One night when Jenny was about four years old, I decided to skip the usual bedtime story and tell her about the day we brought her home from the hospital. The telling so delighted her that it became the most frequently requested bedtime story. When other kids wanted to hear Dr. Seuss, Ferdinand the Bull, or Winnie the Pooh, mine wanted to hear "that one when you got me from the hospital."

I usually began with how exciting it was in 1969 for our family because we were going to have a brand-new baby. We grew impatient waiting to hear when we could get our baby from the doctor. But on February 11 we were in the hospital for only two hours when our sweet little girl arrived. When Daddy came to take us home, she was sleeping peacefully in the hospital cradle. It was a shame that her big brother, Johnny, who was only eight at the time, had to wait downstairs in the lobby. They didn't allow children under twelve to visit hospital rooms in those days. We hurried so he didn't wait too long. They placed the tiny, pink bundle in my arms for the wheelchair ride out. The nurse pushed the chair and Daddy carried the suitcase as the elevator doors opened on the lobby floor. The whole room filled with smiles as a small, blond boy, barely visible behind a huge armload of colorful flowers, struggled to cross the room. When he approached his new baby sister, a wide grin betrayed his awkward attempts to appear casual. He touched her little cheek and handed me the flowers. "Here, Mom," was all he said.

It was always unspeakable joy to watch Jenny's face as she imagined her brother and the flowers.

I recalled how she giggled as I told her that when we got to the car, I handed my two-day-old bundle to Daddy but he couldn't move his arms. Jenny's tiny size and fragility froze him with fear. When no amount of urging could break that paralysis, the nurse came to the rescue and our new family of four was soon in the car for baby's first ride home. The California sun was shining brightly on the splendor of that moment.

Jen giggled again when I told her that Daddy crept along at thirty miles an hour on the 101 freeway leading from Hollywood to our home in the Valley and that he came to a complete stop at every on-ramp. Nothing was going to happen to his baby. We crawled at that pace right into the driveway! The safe arrival home must have given Daddy confidence because he was able to carry our baby to the nursery and place her gently in the cradle.

That home was a little fixer-upper we had moved into the previous month. Since remodeling had just begun, little Jennifer spent the first few years of life lulled to sleep by the drone of electric drills and saws. On that first night home from the hospital, we were talked into letting our new baby sleep in her big brother's room. Johnny was quite convincing when he explained that as the fastest runner in school he could get to me immediately if she cried. With her close by he'd be sure to hear every sound.

That was quite true. Responding to each little noise he was there nudging me awake. Dragging myself out of a much-needed sleep I'd find her still sleeping. I suggested that perhaps he should wait until he heard a good loud cry and then we'd know for certain it was feeding time. I have often pictured little Johnny sitting there all night, eyes glued to the cradle, wondering if it was time.

When it *was* time, he was there helping, handing me diapers, oil, cotton, a blanket, *everything*. It was my practice to preface each request with "Honey, please hand me . . ." and end with "Thank you for helping." Concerned that the extra words created a lack of brevity, he insisted that we forget the "Honey, please" and "thank you," since it would take much less time if I just quickly said "bottle" or "diaper" or "oil." He was very adamant about the new plan. So there we were, mother, big brother, and brand-new baby sister forming a special bond.

In the morning, Johnny went off to school with hair uncombed, teeth not brushed, and worried that I couldn't handle the job alone. That night was pretty much a repeat of the last. The next morning it was hard not to miss the large, dark circles under his eyes even though he tried to stifle the yawns. It was clear that this little third-grader needed sleep more than school that day. He didn't argue when I suggested he go back to bed; in fact, he slept most of the day. The third night we moved the bassinet to the nursery and Johnny didn't say a word.

When I had finished the story Jenny often asked me to tell it "just one more time."

Once again, remembered joy had overtaken my sadness as I recalled the sweet baby smells and sounds that filled the house. February turned into March and things settled into a routine. Middle-of-the-night feedings became our special time when, except for the soft glow of the night-light, the house was dark. It seemed like the whole world was sleeping. As I nursed my baby in the rocking chair, in the silence it felt like little Jenny and I were one. There were times when we both fell asleep and didn't wake until she was ready for the next feeding. That tiny, warm bundle, pressed against my body, was moving herself deeply into my heart and soon became the central focus of our lives. By the end of 1969, Neil Armstrong walked on the moon but it paled next to the miracle that was my family. I was more than grateful that my childhood promise to have a close family one day had been fulfilled.

As the day's journaling ended I was smiling again. It's wonderful to find that happiness, experienced so long ago, still resides deep within. As the sun sank behind the hills that surround the San Fernando Valley, I switched off the word processor.

But before finishing dinner, like a thick fog the sad thoughts rolled in to spoil my joy. The oppressive density of potential loss had returned. I did the dishes, wondering if this despair would ever end for good.

When it was time to go to bed, I lay there in the dark trying to recapture my earlier success at recalling happy memories, but the sadder ones held more weight. A long roller coaster ride had just begun and though I didn't believe it then, this bumpy ride would lead the way out.

It wasn't until the first faint light of morning cast a glow in the room that I drifted off to sleep. When I awoke, sunlight filled the room, but the digital clock announced that only a little more than an hour had passed.

Chapter 3
A RAY
OF HOPE

I N THE BRIGHT LIGHT OF morning the events of the previous day seemed to offer a strong ray of hope. It was clear that writing down an incident from long ago brought back each detail with remarkable clarity as if it were happening again, and the feelings were much the same. Sadness or joy were there in full. In the newness of the day, I found myself wondering if I should go on. This trip back in time had transported me to the house where Little Martha died; reentering that world would be like asking for pain. But if memories continue to live buried within, they must affect the soul on a very deep level and serve as a determining factor in much that we think and do. In that moment I understood more fully than ever before that if this separation from Jen was to make sense, I had to continue. If I stay on this track, long forgotten joy and pain would tell me their secrets and the written word would be my time machine.

I lay there basking in a newfound sense of purpose. Where will I journey today? My thoughts drifted back to the time when my children were little and each day was an unfolding mystery. I recalled feeling responsible and also worried, wanting to provide what my parents couldn't, to prepare them for life as I hadn't been, and to be the positive force that guides their way. But most of all I wanted to return to the joy they brought to me.

Fingering the lace on my pillow, I smiled to remember the time when eighteen-month-old Jenny became our most reliable alarm clock. I welcomed the surge of happiness as I pictured the early morning ritual we shared. She would crawl to our room, climb onto the bed, and kiss our sleeping faces until someone woke up. For a long time that joy started our day.

It was a splendid challenge to have two completely different children with their own unique needs. Johnny, my one treasure from a failed teenage marriage, had been a slender, wiry little baby who learned to scoot around much too early. It came to my attention rather dramatically one day when I left him kicking on the soft living-room rug. I returned just moments later to find his blanket empty. It was a terrifying discovery. How could a six-week-old baby move that fast? After quickly checking the doors and windows, a frantic search of the room produced a happy, squealing baby behind the blue easy chair. He'd managed to scoot some fifteen feet away! That was definitely a harbinger of things to come and the reason I spent the next two years with my son perched on one hip.

Physically advanced and exceptionally bright, no matter how I tried to out-think him, he could somehow climb to the highest shelf and retrieve things that had been placed well out of reach. Johnny's fearless antics led to a succession of accidents that sent us rushing again and again to the emergency room where everyone knew him by name.

In stark contrast, gentle, quiet baby Jennifer was careful, precise, and seldom broke anything. She took her time, preferring to quietly observe. Each step was well thought out and unlike big brother she rarely did anything dangerous. It really surprised me, rounding a corner one day, to find her standing inside a kitchen drawer trying to climb up to the sink. A skullbreaking fall backward was just beginning and there was no hope of reaching her in time to stop the fall. I froze in terror, then watched with utter amazement as she floated like a feather to the floor, touched down lightly, turned over, and crawled away. I leaned against the counter gasping and wondering if what I had just seen had actually happened.

It soon became clear that Jenny's gentle fall was only one of many unusual things that would happen to this quiet baby girl. But now my little girl was a grown woman, needing something still quite unknown to me. Her anger had shaken our relationship like the harsh rattle of a strong earthquake, causing weaknesses in its foundation to be exposed.

With our world now in shambles, I found comfort just lying there recalling the sweetness of being her mother. Another unusual incident came to mind.

Two-year-old Jen had just learned to ride her little red tricycle and loved to pedal around in the yard. One day she let out a loud, hysterical cry and I went racing to the back door. I saw right away that there were no physical injuries yet her convulsive sobbing continued. As the sobs gradually subsided, I understood her to say, "The grass is talking." "Oh," I said. But I never did quite understand *what* it said. Whatever it was, she clearly didn't like it.

It warmed my heart to watch my tough little son hover tenderly over his new baby sister. From the beginning he designated himself to be her protector. When we went to play in the park, he made sure that she had plenty of cool water to drink and that kids didn't throw sand. On outings he was in charge of pointing to everything she needed to see and more. Jen adored her big brother and a great love between them developed.

I continued to lie in bed, holding onto images of two very different children growing up together: the scruffy little blond boy who tested his climbing skills and everyone's patience, and his gentle little sister who floated to the floor like a feather and heard grass talking. They were a constant source of worry but always kept us laughing and totally fascinated.

Is it possible that so significant a part of my life is gone forever? To hide from the fear I pressed my face into the pillow. Was it all going to end with this terrible nightmare?

I wanted to get up but pain held me down. I tried to strike a bargain with it, saying, "If you give me some time off, I'll have a good cry with you later."

The telephone rang and my friend Bari asked how I was doing. The question was enough to make me lose control. In response to my tears, she gently suggested that I make an appointment for a counseling session at church. It had become my practice to take any good suggestion, and, thankfully, the minister squeezed me in.

I told him I'd been thinking about my little sister and was surprised that the memories were so real. He was happy to learn that

I'd been exploring the past and wanted to hear about my feelings. I told him I felt like a failure and that everything I did went wrong. He asked me to consider that Jennifer and I might be too dependent on each other. Whining some more, I replied, "That's not fair. After our divorce her father was never around. I was the only one there. We were bound to be close."

"To invest too much self-worth in your daughter can be a burden for her," the minister said, "especially if it leads to a need to control her."

I balked. "Can it really be that I, who love her so much, would do that?" Deep down inside I didn't buy it.

When it was time to go, he urged me to continue the review of my life. "The past will give you many answers," he said.

On the way home I argued with myself. Nancy, please, this man is trying to help, I thought. But he thinks I'm the only one responsible. What good does it do to blame someone else? I was a good mother! Don't resist.

The idea that Jen had to remove herself from my life was a bitter pill to swallow. And if too much of my self-worth is tied up with motherhood, what can I do about it now? Old feelings, like laundry lint, keep reappearing.

Not ready to return home, I stopped at the market. Standing in line I noticed Jennifer on a magazine cover. Tears dropped from under my sunglasses as I thought about the many times people commented on how alike we are, and that they had never seen it so clearly as when they were watching her on television. Standing there hugging a box of laundry detergent, those remarks that once filled me with pride were now making me feel uneasy. Placing the soap on the register belt I wondered if what people were seeing was evidence that my influence had been too strong.

I bought the magazine. It wasn't purchased with the usual intent of proudly showing it to Jen as proof of how well she was doing. In a way, I had been reduced to fan status, buying a magazine to get news about my daughter.

Driving home I thought about the many people who had expressed happiness for our whole family and showed genuine interest in Jennifer's success. An uneasiness returned. I'd been keeping this terrible separation a closely guarded secret, dreading that disclosure would only increase the unbearable feeling of shame. It was difficult to hide the truth because everyone wanted to know what it was like to have a famous daughter. I prayed it would end soon and there would be no need to explain what I didn't fully understand myself.

I eased my car into the garage and unloaded the grocery bags. For a moment I questioned my ability to survive this thing. Was it a mistake not to call her? Should I apologize for . . . for what? I really didn't know what I had done. An urge to run and hide from the world was inviting but I knew it was out of character. I hadn't run from the "pear lady" had I? Funny to think of that.

Walking to the front door I recalled the time when my sisters and I were little and it was forbidden to pick pears from widow Jones's tree. It was an activity strictly prohibited by Father's pointing finger and confirmed by stern looks from Mother, suggesting consequences too dire to imagine. But when we got a taste for those delicious pears, the warnings usually went unheeded. One time we were happily enjoying the juicy sweetness when the widow, who canned every pear on her tree, came out shaking both fists and yelling to God and everybody. We took off. I turned around to make sure that my youngest sister's chubby little toddler legs had carried her away but saw that the "pear lady" was whacking her bottom. I ran back to rescue Linda and we both got a good licking. When she let us go there was still Mommy and Daddy to face! It was the surprise of our life and a great relief that our parents refrained from further punishment. We "thanked God for his mercy" and gave up pear picking forever.

As I put away the groceries, I realized that from the pear incident I learned a good life-lesson. It was more scary to imagine getting caught than it actually had been. Many times in the years to come that knowledge gave me courage when I had none and strength to tell the truth when lying would have been easier. Now when I need truth more than ever, if I keep focused on what's best for both Jen and me, those qualities will see me through this difficult period as well.

Longing to hear Jennifer's familiar voice, I cursed the empty answering machine. I put the last loaf of bread away and opened the magazine. It was wonderful to find several beautiful pictures, even one with her father. Then an article full of inaccuracies spoiled my pleasure. Was an overzealous employee feeding the press misleading half-truths and bold lies? Or worse, had my daughter actually talked about my past that way? Hurt and angry, I tossed the rag into the trash as I reached for the ringing telephone. Yes, I had just seen it. Yes, I know they made it sound like I didn't raise Jennifer. No, there's nothing I can do. I hung up quickly. My sister meant well, but I needed to process this alone.

My irritation increased as I remembered that celebrities hire people who arrange interviews and tell family members what to say to the press. How ironic. Who is telling *them* what to say about us? Had anyone asked me for the truth about my past? I thought of someone censuring Johnny—the same Johnny who spent the first two nights of Jennifer's life with his eyes glued to the bassinette, afraid that no one would hear her cry. His judgment would have been better than what was appearing in recent articles. It occurred to me that the family needed protecting from *them*.

It was time to rescue myself from this annoyance. I returned to the word processor in an attempt to jog loose some happy memories. As I typed up the recollections from that morning, my annoyance cleared quickly as my thoughts returned to the early seventies, when Jen was about two years old, and to another one of those unusual incidents.

In reaction to a loud burst of giggling I rushed to see what was happening and found my little girl lying facedown and fingering something that was making her laugh. "What do you see that's so funny?" She said she was talking to the Little People. It was obvious that whatever else they were, the "Little People" were invisible. She played like that for nearly an hour and from that day on, a group of these playmates came every day to the same corner of the dining room near the door that lead to the children's bedrooms. Her father and I always knew when they arrived because the house filled with Jenny's infectious laughter. Little visitors played with our baby but were quite unseen by anyone else. John, Johnny, and I accepted it completely, but some of our friends were worried that her sense of reality was threatened.

Jennifer's godmother showed her concern by coming to visit with a small basket of adorable little cloth dolls. The plan was to present them to Jennifer as the *real* Little People, hoping to transfer the imagined ones to the dolls. Jen squealed with delight as she reached for the beautiful basket of dolls. She gave Lynn big thank-you hugs, then ran off to show her wonderful present to the *real* Little People. One day a tragedy occurred that put an end to the problem forever when Daddy walked quickly past the area where the Little People gathered. Baby Jennifer ran in shrieking and crying. Apparently Daddy had stepped right on top of the entire group. You know, they really were invisible! Loud cries and tears told us they had been severely damaged by his big feet and there was no consoling Jen. Being the creative actor he is, John picked them up and stroked them back to health. Jen was happy, but her father, having grown tired of stepping around that area, suggested that we put them in the bathtub to avoid anymore accidents. The little tear-stained face nodded in assent and was right there supervising as he carefully lowered them into the tub.

The Little People didn't come again. Jenny must have known their secret because she never asked about them. John wondered later if they might have gone down the drain.

That delightful memory reminded me of another unusual Jenny moment. I found her standing on the coffee table with arms out like a bird, bending slightly forward. It was apparent by the intense concentration that she believed she could fly and was trying to remember how. I watched from a distance and was intrigued by the small, precise gestures in her upper body. It went on for some time. But when this or that movement didn't accomplish the lift off, she jumped down and ran off. I suppose I should have removed her from the coffee table but the look on her face had me almost convinced. If she *could* fly I wanted to be the first to know.

With each of these incidents, I became more and more aware that this child had a sensitive nature and needed protecting from a world that might not understand her way of seeing things. I was determined to nurture those delightful qualities that were emerging every day.

I became so deeply bonded that her every tumble, every challenge, every disappointment felt as if it happened to me. At just three years of age, a severe headache sent Jenny screaming in agony to our big bed. She writhed in pain, holding her head. I sat there not knowing what to do. Out of desperation I removed her little hands and placed my hand on her forehead. She immediately grabbed hold of my wrist and held on as I felt a surge of the full force of my love. Before long the spasms stopped as her body relaxed and silence replaced the whimpering sounds. I continued to gently caress the pain and if I tried to remove my hand, she pulled it back. After half an hour she let go. The pain was gone! I was amazed and awed by the wonder and protective qualities of a mother's presence. Love that seemed to stream from infinity had brought comfort to my child.

In 1973, Jen turned four and it was time for social interaction with other children. I had read in a brochure about Waldorf Education, which proposes that the key to developing critical thinking is to protect a child's active and creative imagination. It was time to send Jenny to preschool, but I was afraid that the wrong school would interfere with her very active imagination and sensitive nature. There wasn't a school that taught the Waldorf curriculum in our neighborhood and I was unwilling to settle for a less desirable one. I noticed that our church had a large backyard and sun-filled rooms that sat empty during the week. I got the idea to ask our minister if he might consider using that space to open a Waldorf preschool for three mornings a week. He liked the idea.

He and I made several trips to government agencies in Los Angeles to find out what was needed to meet the legal requirements. After hours of paperwork and visits from city officials, we complied with the necessary codes. Reverend Walter hired a teacher who had formerly taught the Waldorf method. I became director of enrollment and set to work finding students. Parents were happy to hear that their child would be appreciated for his or her unique qualities and would feel protected in the homey atmosphere that the pedagogy embraces. We opened for business. A feature of the curriculum in the early grades is to have the teacher read fairy tales after which the story is acted out by the children. Each child takes a different part, one time pretending to be a big bad wolf and the next a trusting Little Red Riding Hood. Jenny's first experience with acting happened in this play enjoyed by all of the children. In this wholesome atmosphere my growing daughter experienced life away from home.

The day had flown by and it was nearing dusk. Stretching with pleasure, I thought of the variety of lovely images that had returned to remind me that life is truly wonderful. It was magnificent to find that once again happy times, relived fully, replaced the sadness of missing Jennifer and Johnny. I put the journal away.

While preparing a small supper for myself I had the distinct impression that, somehow, the past was healing the present as images passed through my mind in a parade of life's substance. I was walking that thin line between joy and pain and if loneliness caused me to stray too far from the line, I was gaining the capacity to move myself back. Could this be the path to a place I'd never been?

As the weight of my body sank into bed, I felt a resurgence of hope. For the first time in many weeks I fell quickly and deeply asleep.

Chapter 4
TRANS-
FORMATION

I LAY THERE LISTENING TO the rain. To wake well-rested was a moment worth savoring. Glancing around I flinched at the clutter. My fastidious nature had succumbed to emotional upheaval and I hadn't even bothered to empty the ashtrays. Everywhere I looked there was disarray and chaos. It was time to do a major housecleaning. I threw back the down quilt, eager to get started.

The stench of stale cigarettes filled the room. Smoking had never been a habit, though I did use it occasionally for stress. In recent weeks, from the looks of the ashtrays, it had gotten quite out of hand. I pushed back the curtain and opened the window. The rain had eased to a drizzle, leaving the air smelling sweet and fresh. On the way to the kitchen I set out the vacuum cleaner.

Waiting for coffee to brew, I could feel a pain deep within that told me Reverend Jim was right: I must continue this process of reflection. This separation was important for both me and Jen. It wasn't easy to admit that others had seen what I hadn't. With new insights coming every day, I couldn't yet assess the full potential for gain, but it was clear that because of this terrible estrangement I would reach a new level of understanding of myself and of Jennifer. I mused that when the heart is suffering the mind can't come to its rescue. My good sleep had restored the mind that had deserted me for the last several months and things were making sense.

I ran water to extinguish a cigarette, tossed the butt in the trash, and poured coffee. Resisting another temptation to call Jen, I turned with newfound vigor to tackle the mess.

I felt somehow resurrected. Reborn. After walking around in a deathlike state, I had awakened feeling as if I were once again among the living. The vacuum cleaner hummed on.

I thought of the shock it had been when, in 1980, Jennifer's father quite suddenly ended our marriage. It had taken a long time to recover from the blow and although I hadn't become one of those embittered women, I often wondered if some unresolved feelings from that experience didn't allow me to really let go and trust men. Encouraged by the healing that was coming from making an ever more detailed retrospective of my life, I decided it was time to delve into that issue. The mindless activity of cleaning house allowed a stream of memories to flow in.

It seemed like yesterday. I was only twenty-four when my teenage marriage failed and I became a single mom, raising my three-year-old son alone. A small amount of support from my ex-husband helped, but I was also accepting modeling jobs to make ends meet while I prepared to become an actress myself. One of the men I'd been dating surprised me with a marriage proposal.

54

He was attractive and wealthy. After a childhood of poverty it was all too tempting. But a tall, handsome, Greek actor had stolen my heart. He was a quiet, gentle man named John Aniston, with strong family values, and he seemed incapable of hurting anyone. Three years after our first date, we married and my son once again had a proper, stable family. Life wouldn't be easy because John hadn't a penny. The year was 1965 and flower children were everywhere, bringing their message of love. Ours was a love strong enough to carry the challenge of the future together. We shared a sense of humor that would sustain us through the darkest of times. He was wonderful with my son and that was more important than anything to me.

As the months passed, it turned out that my husband seldom worked. I found it increasingly difficult to watch while my own career was advancing. I lacked John's collegiate training and experience in the theater, yet I was being cast in better roles. It just wasn't fair. We had complete confidence in John's talent but suspected that his swarthy good looks, and a broken nose he had suffered in childhood, probably gave casting people their often-stated narrow view that John was only right to play gangster roles. Typecasting was, and still may be, a wicked little practice. We repeatedly told each other that one good part would prove them wrong, and we'd just have to be a little more patient.

Even though time passed and John still couldn't jump-start his career, it just wasn't my nature to sit around and do nothing. I knew that if an agent wasn't able to produce good parts, the actor will sometimes hire a manager whose job is to give them a more marketable image. A skilled manager can help an actor achieve a star-quality appearance the way studios did in the old days. Why couldn't I? I began a careful analysis to determine what we might do.

My guy was a talented actor and to me he was perfectly beautiful, but I knew that in this business a look that appeals to the masses can be even more important than talent to get a career started. I determined that some minor repairs to correct the poorly healed break in his nose would also help correct breathing problems he had suffered since childhood. A more current hairstyle, cosmetic dental work, shedding twenty pounds, and some new clothes would definitely make a big difference at auditions.

Before mentioning it to John, some serious questions needed to be answered. How could we finance this makeover? Would he misunderstand? Would I hurt his feelings and in the process our marriage? As time passed, with his career stuck in neutral and no prospects for improvement, I had to take the chance.

I was relieved to find that after some initial resistance he saw my point and accepted the idea with his usual good humor. We made jokes about the risk to his appearance and got silly imagining how he might end up looking. John was nervous about the change but eventually, like all couples working together to bring something about, we gathered our courage and decided to give it a try. With a little money I'd stashed away, we did as good a job as any major studio or high-priced manager. The change to his appearance was so impressive that a couple of our male friends asked me to do the same for them.

John looked fantastic but we were both disappointed when his agent still couldn't book him a decent audition. I worried that with John now well past thirty, the change may have come too late for California's youth-oriented market. Our only stable income continued to be a small amount of support I received from Johnny's father and our occasional jobs. John said he planned to find some kind of work to tide us over. An old friend, also an actor, was selling real estate and suggested that John look into it as well. When John received his real-estate license, our mood was jubilant as he went out to sell his first tract of homes. We were confident that our finances were about to improve. It didn't happen. People weren't buying those houses and John soon gave up. I suggested that he find a more stable source of income. Like many struggling actors, he reasoned that a regular job might entice him away from acting.

Though life was difficult we still managed to get by. John had learned to survive on his meager earnings before we married and the severe poverty I knew as a child prepared me for tough times. Still, there was our absolute faith in John's talent. The sacrifices would one day be forgotten.

I was annoyed with my agent, Peter. He was grooming me for stardom in a way that violated my view of women. Peter was impressed by the way Marilyn Monroe's sexy image helped her succeed and he was sure I could do the same. We had been arguing for weeks. The latest offense was over his suggestion that instead of a bikini I wear a lacy bra and panties to interviews. Actors are often asked to be seen in swimsuits and that was his tawdry idea of varying the theme. When it was time for me to be seen I was to say, "Oh dear, I forgot," then suggest that if they don't mind, undies aren't much different than a swimsuit. I was to demurely say, "I don't mind if you don't." The thought of doing anything so tacky made me furious and I told him so. It was 1967 and social conventions were being overturned. Public nudity was no longer a rarity. Peter criticized my views as being outdated and said that I needed to think it over because he wasn't interested in representing me if I wouldn't cooperate.

The next day I had an appointment with a producer at Paramount Studios. A car and a driver were waiting at the studio gate to escort me on the long drive to the producer's office. A rather tall, dignified, older gentleman with kind gray eyes was just leaving as the secretary ushered me in. We were introduced as he left. The interview with the producer went well and to my surprise, that older gentleman was waiting for me in the hall. He was an agent and he wondered if I needed one. He patiently listened as I told him about my problems with Peter. He said he had never heard of anything so terrible. He said if I was that unhappy, I should sign with him.

That's how Sam Armstrong became my new agent and I was greatly relieved to be rid of the constant pressure to do something I had no intention of doing. I could just imagine how my father would react if his daughter became a sex kitten. Never mind that *I* hated the idea, as long as my dad was alive it wasn't even a question.

John and I had been married three years. One day when I returned home, exhausted from standing for hours under hot lights on cement floors, I realized that it had become increasingly common to find that John had slept all morning and had spent the rest of the day watching television. I couldn't complain because he would have gladly changed places. It was hell to live like that and I knew we couldn't go on. In my mind there was only one thing to do. It was the summer of 1968, and I had just discovered we were about to have a baby. I decided then and there that the best thing for our family would be for me to give up my career. John, believing that any day his career would take off, didn't resist my decision.

Sam Armstrong, a real old-world gentleman like my dad, had worked hard on my career, but he didn't say a cross word or try to change my mind. He respected my wish to be a full-time mother and understood that I had no desire to compete with my husband.

My decision added to our shortage of money, but with a child on the way, there wouldn't be room for our growing family in what had been my apartment before we married. So with a loan from my father we managed to buy a small bank foreclosure that had been on the market for several years. The bank had done nothing to enhance its appearance but the neighborhood was good, the lot was big, and the price was very low. To us that sad-looking little house had potential. John said his father had taught him to build things and I had a talent for decorating on a shoe-string. A monumental transformation began.

I was winding the cord to put the vacuum away when I recalled that soon after the baby came, John's work had all but dried up and things were getting very bad. But there was a lot to be done to make our house livable, and it became a daily intrigue to find a way to get what we needed to do the job.

I was the designer/decorator and John did most of the hard work himself. He amazed everyone with the skills he'd learned as a child and, later, building sets in summer stock.

Making our pennies stretch to get supplies was a constant pressure that pushed our imaginations to the edge. John remembered that in New York out-of-work actors furnish their cold water flats by scouting around the city looking for things people put on the street for trash pick-up. In this way we even found some discarded four-by-fours to use for ceiling beams, which added charm to our house. Used supplies, including lumber, were picked up for change and helped make our home a reality.

For months plastic tarps hung across the back of the house to keep the elements out while walls and windows were being transformed. Taking care of a new baby and a growing boy with the house torn apart was challenging. Our bed in the living room made socializing impossible as we juggled our finances to keep it going. But despite all that, there was always something to laugh about. Humor helped get us through some trying times.

But as the months dragged on with very few acting auditions, it became difficult to motivate John to put in a full day of work on the house. He preferred to sleep until noon and I started to lose my patience.

I was surprised that remembering the old frustration so many years later would still fill me with irritation. I went outside to shake the area rugs. The sun was out and the patch of sky above my condo was a deep, rich blue. Dust from the rugs flew in the sunlight as I recall wishing that I had more patience to get through those trying times.

After returning the rugs, I began to dust the antiques collected during the days when even John and I found some that were affordable. When the remodeling was almost done, one of my jobs had been to supply the finishing touches.

We were introduced to the magical world of swap meets. And magic it was. Everyone was sleeping as I crept out of the house at six o'clock on Sunday mornings. Heirlooms were waiting to be purchased for pennies; the secret was to arrive ahead of the crowds. I rarely scraped together more than ten dollars, but often returned home with the back seat loaded. John stayed home with the kids. When I returned, he would rush out to see the treasures from my hunt.

I smiled as I reflected on the pride of watching our house become more and more beautiful. To see so little turn into so much was astounding. It was truly modern alchemy. We delighted at the surprised reactions of friends who said we were nuts to buy that "dump."

As I continued dusting the lovely pieces, my thoughts drifted back to an incident in my own childhood that may have started my passion for antiques. I was just five years old but the memory is still vivid.

A kind, older woman named Mrs. Miller lived next door. She would help our family by coming over to check on us when my parents were both at work. (Today this would be viewed as child neglect but things were different then. Not too many generations earlier, the main reason people had children was to help with chores.) Mrs. Miller was friendly to children and for the first time, one day, she invited me into her apartment. I felt a sensation of pleasure looking at all the beautiful things in her living room. I can still see the brocade couch, large and heavy in contrast to our flimsy one that my sisters and I moved around to play house. There was a matching chair with crocheted doilies, lovely framed pictures on the walls, and a colorful oriental rug under the coffee table. I was enchanted when she showed me the beveled glass cabinet full of lovely figurines and how the crystal lamps caught the light. I had never seen anything so beautiful.

Since I was only five, making a house beautiful was something I had never thought about. When I got home, I took a good look around. Our living room was nearly empty. Instead of a colorful carpet there was dark industrial asphalt tile with a brown tweed couch at one end and a wooden desk with matching chair at the other. Obviously Mommy hadn't thought about it either. I decided to surprise everyone and do it myself. I managed to slide the couch to the opposite wall and dragged six wooden chairs from the kitchen and placed them at the same smart angle as Mrs. Miller had hers. I then covered everything with colorful clothes. Mother's flowered dress became the missing rug, our matching red plaid raincoats covered four of the chairs, and Father's light gray coat looked better on the couch with those white kitchen napkins for doilies. I drew a few pictures for the walls. It was hard to make our house look as beautiful as Mrs. Miller's, but in my eyes it came close.

Mother was furious when she saw "the terrible mess" I'd made. She didn't calm down until everything was put away. I wondered how many times I might have reacted with the same insensitivity to my own children. Without realizing it or intending to, had I caused them similar disappointment?

With the dusting finished, I went into the kitchen to tackle more weeks of neglect. Washing dishes always stimulates a flood of memories and mine returned to that time when my children were young.

Money was so tight that Jennifer didn't have a new piece of clothing for the first few years of her life. Fortunately it was the custom to share outgrown children's clothes with family or friends and we were given three years' supply of beautiful baby clothes. Broke as we were, Jenny was always dressed like a princess. With the added weight of childbirth, I no longer fit into my model-sized clothes. I found myself grumbling about having nothing to wear. My best friend, Molly Reynolds, offered a wonderful, long A-line shift that hid the weight, then she helped me cut a pattern out of tissue paper so we could make two more. I wore those three dresses everywhere, even after the weight came off. We were surviving the odds.

Little Johnny, who was eleven and growing, was not so lucky. He was beginning to look a bit tattered. I felt bad when I saw his worn shoes and patched pants, but he didn't seem to notice. He found it exciting to watch our household renovations going on, especially when he was asked to help with important things like holding the other end of heavy boards (my job during school hours). After living with a single parent, he was happy to have a family.

One day I was filling out a chair with my newly acquired girth when little Johnny came home from school. My position in that chair somehow caused him to notice my weight gain. He flew into my lap and snuggled there. After a moment he said, "This is what a mother should look like." It was clear that my son had not appreciated my model's physique.

Everyone looked forward to the yearly visit of John's mother. Yaya★ cooked wonderful Greek dishes for us, but it was embarrassing when she insisted on buying all of the food. She said it made her happy, but I knew that she had already helped pay our mortgage. I had to admit that her generosity made it possible for us to continue working on the house and I really appreciated the help, but I secretly hated how much it was needed.

Once a friend wanted a cooking lesson from Yaya and she was happy to oblige. After the lesson we all thoroughly enjoyed a fantastic Greek meal, despite the half-finished house.

Baby-sitters were not in the budget but we'd grown used to only going places with the children. During one of Johnny's visits with his biological father, Yaya urged us to accept an invitation to a party in Hollywood. We tried to have fun but an hour or so into

---

★A Greek term of endearment for grandmother.

the evening it felt like something was missing. We wondered in unison if baby Jennifer was okay. I reached for my purse as we both said, "Let's go home." It was our first time away from Jen and we missed her. At home we stood in the hallway light, gazing into the crib, and I saw John's fatherly pride blend with love and radiate from his eyes. As if having heard our silent wish, our baby stood up, ready to play. After a good romp she went right back to sleep and two satisfied parents went to bed happy. Years later, when John's long absence after our divorce caused Jennifer to doubt her father's love, I told her that story. She smiled and felt reassured.

Kids are oblivious to hardships and ours continued to thrive and grow. As Jenny got older she loved to sit with her big brother and watch old reruns of black-and-white television shows. One day she asked me very seriously, "Mommy, in the old days when you were young, was everything in black and white?"

The day came when John's longtime agent grew weary of trying to find work for his client. He didn't want to sign John again when their contract expired. John tried to get another agent but had no luck. The rejection might have been too painful because he soon gave up looking for someone else to represent him.

By 1971, we had been renovating for three years and things were hitting a new low. John and I had been married almost seven years and his hopes and dreams of a career seemed more out of reach than ever before. It had been a long time since he'd had any kind of acting job and for the last year he had no agent. Despite all we'd done in the early months of our marriage, with no agent, prospects for work were nil. I felt unimaginable frustration. It was hard to accept that such a handsome, talented actor wasn't working.

A kind of inertia had settled into John and it was taking all of my will to get him motivated to work on the house. Every nail had to be driven by the combination of his hand and my will. The pressure was becoming too much. A normally quiet man, John sank even further into himself and I began to explode with fits of rage. I feared becoming like my father and hated myself as I begged for forgiveness. John always reassured me that he did forgive me because he knew things weren't easy.

Too much togetherness and not enough diversion from worry for too many years was wearing on us. I made more of an effort to take the kids to the park or to visit friends. One of our favorite outings was to visit my best friend, Molly. Her son, Eric, and my Johnny were buddies and had a great time swimming in her pool and teasing Jennifer. It was hard for a little girl to choose between hanging out with us moms and the dog or taking torment from the boys.

A formerly successful model, Molly was married to an actor, William Reynolds. People often likened her to Elizabeth Taylor, but her inner beauty was even more exquisite. We were both women who shared a determination to be full-time moms. It was the late sixties and Bill was costarring with Ephram Zimbalist Jr. on the long-running TV show *The FBI*. In every way, he supported Molly's view of motherhood. Aware that few actors have Bill's success, Molly had cautioned me that life with an unemployed actor would be tough. But she never judged me for ignoring her advice to reconsider, and she never became impatient when years passed and the financial difficulties didn't let up. On the rare occasions when I needed to vent about John's lethargy, she listened without comment or agreed that children do need a family.

After one of our visits, Molly placed a brown grocery bag in my hand. She said, "This meat will spoil if someone doesn't eat it soon." She asked me to take it because everyone in her house wanted Chinese. I fixed several meals with that hamburger, and Molly made me feel like I had done her a favor.

Molly's friendship was a haven for me. I was nineteen when we met and that meeting turned into a friendship that spanned more than thirty years. I never knew anyone who didn't love Molly. Her endearing kindness and gentle good manners made everyone want to be in her presence. She cast a splendor on the darkest of moments and was there for many who suffered. The main gesture of her being was to make others feel good. In the light and warmth of her love, my own life was infinitely blessed.

Jenny adored Molly and was always eager to spend time at her house. When Molly's children were grown and living with friends or were off at college, she would ask Jenny to spend the night. What a treat! Jenny was allowed to experiment with her makeup and fingernail polish.

Molly and I had a perfectly matched sense of humor and found something funny in almost everything. Even when times were bleak, she would make a comment that was so absurd that I had to top it with something even more outrageous and we'd collapse into fits of convulsive laughter. An afternoon with her was like therapy.

Jen once said that as a child she always thought that if anything ever happened to me, Molly would be there. Instead, we were there for each other when a wicked cancer prematurely ended Molly's life.

As I put the last dish away, I wondered how Molly would advise me to handle this terrible separation from Jen. I missed them both very much.

The day turned out to be warm and clear. The house was spotless and my sore body was proof that I had accomplished a lot. I sank into a chair and lit a cigarette. It had been a day of hard work and remembering. Somehow those memories elevated my feeling of worth.

I must have drifted off to sleep because it was dark when I awoke and my cigarette was out. It might take some doing to become reacquainted with times nearly forgotten, but I felt that on this foundation a whole new life was being built.

Chapter 5
THE HEART REMEMBERS

THE CLOCK RADIO WOKE ME from a second full night's sleep with its forecast of clear skies, bright sun, and cool temperatures. The tidy room coming slowly into focus brought the usual satisfaction and consummate order to my soul. I stretched into the sensation of pleasure.

Then, like a wave pounding the shore, reality hit. For a brief moment I had forgotten the threat of losing Jen and that Johnny still hadn't returned my calls. I was tumbling once again into that gaping black hole of despair. Rolling over to bury tears in my pillow, I wondered if I was destined to be another statistic, to live for years or forever wondering about my kids. Waves seemed to wash away hope. Wait, I said to myself, it's a long, hard climb from the depths of despair, don't fall back now. Johnny will call and time apart from Jen is what we both need. I reached for a tissue.

Besides, it's Thursday and *Friends* will be on tonight! That's a big stretch from her actual presence, but a taped image is better than no Jen at all. Blowing hard I thought about those poor mothers who don't even know where their daughters are or even if they're alive. I headed for the kitchen.

Sipping black coffee, I thought about Molly. How sad that she died so young. Many times I have wished she were here. I missed our long talks when we would laugh about things. I just wanted to feel her presence as I had for so many years. The ringing phone interrupted my longing. My good friend David was calling from New York to express concern for me. He had read an article about Jen. "It refers to you as an unfulfilled, bitter old woman and I know that's not true," he said. I was thinking to myself *not again* when he asked, "Why would they say that?"

"Because these stories sell magazines and if they have nothing nasty to say, they make it up. They don't seem to care or under-stand how helpless you feel or how painful it is to read that you failed in the eyes of your daughter."

"Try not to let it bother you. Jen knows better and so do your friends."

I lit a cigarette and inhaled a full mouth of smoke, trying to ignore the disquieting thought that Jen may have said those things. I preferred to blame it on the press. "Probably just some publicist selling a story."

David pointed out that it's good for Jen to have publicity and no one believes that stuff anyway, then insisted that it was time I stop smoking.

Returning the phone to its cradle, I thought that while the success of *Friends* assured visual access to Jen, it's infuriating to read lies about yourself in the press, and I didn't buy the idea that no one believed it. It seems like my daughter's fame was a double-edged sword. I headed for the word processor to enter the memories from yesterday and to rummage around for some happy ones to replace this annoyance.

Leaning back in the chair, I thought about my son. Why hadn't Johnny returned my calls? Did he understand his sister's actions? I could agree that a neutral position was best until things return to normal. He probably wouldn't call. Thinking about the past had me wondering if after Jenny was born he might have felt a little left out. When the newness wore off, he must have noticed how much more attention the baby required. It hadn't occurred to me before because he never said anything except for that time he confided, rather offhandedly, "Don't worry, Mom, I know you love me as much as her."

I have an old wound of regret that Johnny's school days weren't as happy as Jen's. It was unfortunate for all of us that teachers hadn't yet discovered how to deal with a precocious, hyperactive child. Learning came too easy to Johnny and his attention often wandered, so he disrupted the class. In a crowded public school the best they could do was dismiss his lack of attention as a learning disability. They concluded this about a child who taught himself to read! This was a discovery I made as we did the grocery shopping together.

He was safely perched in the toddler seat as we moved through the aisles. He would ask how to say various letters on food packaging and would then repeat the sound. When we returned home, I'd sit him up on the counter for safekeeping and he'd hand me grocery items to put away. One day he pointed to a letter and asked, "How does that sound?" I made the sound "Wuh." He responded with, "Wuh-wuh-ee, Wheaties?" After

71

that, at just three years old, he could read. Yet, a few years later, professional school teachers failed to understand that he needed more challenging assignments and classified him as a slow learner.

He entered sixth grade with the same bias on his record. One day his science teacher assigned the class projects to do at home. Johnny decided to build a model of the planet Mars. Big John found a large three-by-four-foot board for the base and for days Johnny spent hours of top-secret work behind the closed door to his bedroom. No one was allowed to enter. When it was finished, we were summoned to see the unveiling. It was an exact replica. We were amazed that he'd actually succeeded without once asking for help. He wondered if we thought the teacher would like it enough to give him an A and John helped him carry it to school.

We were more than surprised when a sad face came home from school that day.

The startling news was that the teacher didn't believe Johnny had built his model without the help of a parent and would only grade it a C. When we went to set the record straight with the teacher, he wouldn't believe us either! We insisted. But he wouldn't budge from his mistrust, saying, "A sixth-grade child couldn't do that well alone. Sorry."

Later, when I tried to comfort my little guy, he thought it over and said, "Mom, don't worry. I think the teacher's doubt is better than an A."

When it was time to graduate they weren't sure if this "slow learner" was ready for junior high, so they decided to have him tested. I brought a very nervous little boy to an office where he was given a battery of tests. When the results came back showing a near-genius IQ, we realized that Johnny had nearly dropped through the cracks. I wanted to tear the school apart, but the woman who administered the tests said that my complaint would be a blotch on Johnny's record that would follow him through high school. She advised me to let it go. I did.

Those were the years when John and I faced terrible financial problems on a daily basis, which affected our life in many ways. We couldn't maintain a social life when groceries for the most modest dinner with a couple of friends depleted our entire week's budget. We didn't like accepting invitations that we couldn't return and usually declined. Some of our friends fell away, but there were others who wouldn't take no for an answer and remained close through the years. Lynn and Telly Savalas were among them.

From our first meeting Lynn and I felt an immediate connection. We both came from a New England background and had been taught similar values. Telly's fame placed her in the midst of famous people, privilege, and a stunning home in Beverly Hills. A woman of strong character, Lynn was completely unaffected by her status as the wife of a movie star. I admired her uncomplicated view of life; no matter what, one must always do the right thing. It reminded me of my father.

We both had Greek husbands and Greek mothers-in-law, so there was plenty to talk about. A school teacher by profession, Lynn shared my passion for learning. We spent hours over coffee, discussing our enchantment with Greek culture or interpreting unfamiliar behavior patterns. We always came to the conclusion that it was the Magic-of-Greece thing. In retrospect, I think it was simply the "Men-Are-from-Mars" thing that kept us intrigued. Through our common interests, we built a strong and lasting friendship.

John had taught me to play bridge when we were dating and

Lynn and Telly were passionate players, too. The four of us held many all-night sessions playing this wonderfully addicting game. It added to the fun that Telly would only play for money and refused to give up the "bid." Sitting passively just to keep us from scoring was torture for him. Telly so disliked that defensive position that he often outbid us with fewer than the required twelve points in his hand and we constantly defeated his contract. We'd double for extra score and he'd redouble just to be ornery, insuring us even more. Poor Lynn sat through countless games watching her partner "go down." There were times when Telly bid for the contract with only five points in their combined hands! He'd say to Lynn, "I thought you had more." The four of us laughed until tears ran down our cheeks.

Two magnificent little Savalas girls were upstairs sleeping— that is, unless they found the courage to tiptoe halfway down to crouch on the stairs and watch through the banister, their little faces pressed between the bars to see across the enormous parlor and into the game room at the far end. Candace and Penelope huddled on the staircase, trying to muffle their giggles until Telly, not wanting to tarnish his image as a strict disciplinarian, pretended to scold and then grinned as he motioned for them to join us. I can picture clearly two matching nightgowns streaking across that expanse, big eyes shining as they jumped into Papa's lap, asking, "What's so funny?" They would entertain us with delightful chatter, until Papa grew restless to play another hand and sent them off to bed; for good this time.

Telly was eager to return to the play, saying, "Okay, no more nice guy." We'd deal another hand, the game usually ending in our favor again. This went on all night until we saw the early light of dawn. I'd insist that it was time to collect our winnings and head for the valley. At just a penny a point it was amazing how many pennies we took home. The last fun of the evening was to tease Telly about how much he had helped our budget.

The streets were empty on the drive back to the valley as the first hint of light cast the trees black as night against the sky, and everything seemed peaceful in the soft glow of morning. There was always a replay of events as John and I boasted about our brilliant finesse and recounted the silly things that made us laugh. Yaya and our children were sleeping soundly when we got home.

It was during one of those evenings that Telly brought up the topic of Jennifer's baptism. She was nearly two years old and it was about time. He pointed out that being best man at our wedding, in Greek tradition, entitled him to be godfather. After a rather playful discussion, we all agreed that for many reasons Lynn and Telly would be perfect godparents for our precious baby.

Plans had to be made but none of us really knew what needed to be done, so Lynn and I frequently consulted with our respective mothers-in-law. Mana (Telly's mom) told us that baptism is so serious that the parties involved become joined like a family even to the point of beginning to look alike. Yaya told us that the child's clothing had to be entirely removed during the ceremony and replaced with a new set from the godparents. I thought maybe it was a gesture to claim her as theirs. With our heads full of unfamiliar things like special almonds, wheat berries sweetened with sugar and cinnamon, baptism cross, and the like, we two all-American women managed to plan the event.

The big day finally came.

Almost everything went well. Telly held Jenny through the ceremony and managed to keep her from crying by whispering secrets in her ear. He even coaxed her to drink the Holy wine. Little

Johnny squirmed in the pew, nervously biting well-chewed finger-nails as he wondered what would happen next to his sister. Lynn carried our baby to the dressing room to be changed into new baptism clothes. Both smiled all the way. When they emerged, Lynn not only held a beautifully dressed Jennifer, but a firm commitment to be a wonderful godmother, and indeed she was.

Candace and Penelope fell right into their roles as godsisters, as our hearts and minds shifted from friends to family.

After the ceremony, Jen and I were to ride in the Savalases' car to their house where people were gathering to celebrate. Apparently the excitement and the wine had upset Jenny's tummy and before Telly could hand her to me in the backseat, a good portion of her breakfast landed on his black velvet lapel. She sat on my lap for the drive to Beverly Hills and shot the remainder of that breakfast all over me and the backseat of her new godfather's Rolls.

When we arrived at their house, Nouno (Greek for "godfather") changed his clothes and Lynn loaned me something of hers. Upon hearing what happened, Yaya feared that the holy wine would be desecrated, so we carefully blotted up the vomit, gathered our soiled clothes, and packed everything in plastic to take home.

Squealing cousins played in the big backyard. Jen was too young to play, but Candace and Penelope fiercely protected their newly christened godsister. Johnny wondered why he didn't have godparents. From a distance, he kept a watchful eye on his little sister as he played with the older boys.

Later, at home, Yaya washed the soiled garments in a large plastic tub and poured the water into the rose garden to prevent the sacred fluid from entering the contaminated Los Angeles sewer system. Everyone admired Yaya's religious dedication.

I stretched my stiff back and recalled that as the years passed, shy Penelope, with her large, intelligent brown eyes and gentle manner, had found a special place in my heart. One day we made a pact that I could be her second godmother, a role I embrace with great joy. It was a real blessing for me and Jennifer when, years later, we ended up living in Manhattan on the same street as Penelope.

I let the word processor fall into power save and felt the stiffness in my back. I headed for the kitchen to scavenge around for a bite of lunch. As a can of soup twirled in the can opener, I was smiling. Happy memories had replaced the morning's sadness.

Lunch was over, the dishes were done, and my thoughts were still full. Is it the heart that remembers? I returned to the word processor, still warmed by thoughts about the Savalas family.

Like many women in her position, Lynn might have turned the care of her children over to a nanny. But Lynn preferred to be the one to raise her children (another view we had in common). She often brought her girls to our house to play. It was a special kind of fun to be there with John building our house in the background. Lynn and I were always willing to give our opinions, but we also pitched in with physical help. Once we learned how to lay used red brick in carefully prepared sand for the patio floor. John showed us how to place the bricks in alternate directions and as the bricks were laid, we watched the basket-weave pattern appear. When painful little red dots showed up on our fingertips, we learned what strawberries were. We joked that if times got tough for Telly, Lynn could get work as a bricklayer.

A magnificent oak tree stood in the far corner of our back-yard. Johnny wanted to build a tree house there, so big John saved a pile of discarded wood and taught him how to use a hammer and nails. Our fair-haired little carpenter managed to build a wonderful "structure" in the arms of that gigantic oak and many boyhood dreams were spun in the breeze that drifted through its long branches.

The tree house became Johnny's private sanctuary, and when Penelope and Candace were invited up to play, their big brown eyes sparkled with joy. It was an opportunity too golden to miss. Jenny was much too little to climb a tree and came running to announce, "They won't play with me!"

The dark cloud of worry and financial pressure overshadowed all that was good in our lives. Years were passing and I began to fear that John had serious problems with earning a living. I found myself nagging again. An actor friend who worked selling insurance arranged for John to get a job with his company. We were surprised to find that John's territory covered such a large area. He would set out in the morning and drive all day to the houses of prospective clients. I would wait with great anticipation for him to come home with the news of a sale. There were few. He said he often felt pressure to sell insurance to people who didn't need it. His sales were meager and after trying for weeks, he gave up. I felt bad for him, but actors often find themselves working at all sorts of odd jobs until the big break comes. John's heart just wasn't in it. Eventually he refused to do anything but act. I ran out of patience. One day I bellowed, at the top of my lungs, "Why do you think you're the only man who doesn't have to sup-port his family?" My voice was full of rage.

I wanted to get a job but I believed that John's nature wasn't suited to take care of children for extended periods of time. There was a close call when Jen, just a toddler, managed to push a large bowl from a side table in the dining room. While John's attention was elsewhere, our curious baby went exploring. I came home to find shards of jagged porcelain that had once been an old washbasin. A wave of terror passed over me. Jenny might have really been hurt! After that, when John was alone with the kids I worried. It never happened again, but I felt he wasn't cut out to be Mr. Mom. For me, working was not an option because child care would have taken all of my salary, and, unlike my own mother, I wanted to be there for my kids. We were in a bind; John wouldn't do anything but act and I had to take care of the children.

The renovations to the house were nearly finished and without an agent, John had no hope of finding work. We'd been married about six years, his career was more out of reach than we'd ever imagined, and I feared that even if John did get an audition, his confidence would be so shaken that it wouldn't go well. An actor needs energy to perform and nothing is more depleting than need. I needed some advice.

My friend Dodi was a good source. She was married to a successful film producer and before that she had worked in the movie business for years. She often impressed me with her insightful words. Dodi obliged and came over with a treat for lunch. After the usual greetings she said, "Sit down, let's talk."

When I finished my carefully worded dilemma she said, "Don't get mad, but I've got to ask, why doesn't he get a regular job?"

Dodi was one of those valuable friends who would always tell you the truth. I knew how much she cared about me and the kids. I tried to explain, saying, "Dodi, he's working hard on the house and it's just a matter of time."

Dodi wasn't convinced. "How many years can you wait?" she asked as tears filled my eyes. "You're crying. I don't mean to upset you but look, he's still sleeping and it's past noon. Why can't he get a job in the morning?"

"He's tried! But his talent is acting! What I need is some advice on how to get his career going."

Dodi stepped into the opening. "Wake up! He's almost forty, and you're wasting your youth and your beauty!"

"But, we have a family here. I know what it's like to live without one. I won't do that to my kids."

Dodi urged me to calm down. Then she mumbled that if it hadn't been for my deprived childhood, I'd never have married a man with such a poor history of work and probably would have found that wealthy man's proposal more appealing.

"Dorothy, you know I love John and one day his career will take off. I would never marry for money!"

Dodi continued, "I hate to disillusion you, but I know the business and a person that passive isn't likely to have a career. My first husband was like John and I had to yell to get him to do anything. When I learned about passive aggression, I asked him for a divorce. To this day he's done nothing with his life."

"Yeah, I do a lot of yelling, too," I said. But I didn't want Dodi to push it too far, saying, "John is not like your ex-husband and things are bound to change soon."

"But you—"

"C'mon, you," I said, "let's eat lunch."

It seems that I inherited my mother's migraine headaches. After years of unsuccessfully trying to find a cure, they were becoming more severe and more frequent. When painkillers didn't help,

John would massage my head and shoulders to get the muscles to relax. It never failed to amaze us when he found a knot that would yield to the pressure and make the pain disappear. There was magic in my husband's hands. As time passed, with or without a headache, it became a wonderful bedtime habit to watch television or read with my head on his chest as the gentle massage put me to sleep. The stress from a day of worry about the future was eased. That night, John, without knowing it, pressed Dodi's words out of my mind.

But I knew it was up to me to think of something. An idea had been forming. John was always eager to clean wounds or take temperatures if anyone got sick, and he was fascinated to read about surgical procedures. He regularly described, in great detail, the joy of watching his friend, a surgeon, perform operations. People often commented that John would make a wonderful doctor. Apparently an aptitude test he had taken in college confirmed it.

John was in the last group eligible to receive the GI Bill, which paid the tuition and a small amount of support money for veterans returning to school. Maybe if he went back to college to study medicine, it would bolster his ego, offer a more promising profession, and we could certainly use the three hundred dollars a month.

I had been wanting to present my idea to John but dreaded his customary resistance. The house was now finished and something had to be done. I bit the bullet and spelled out my plan. He was deadset against it, saying, "I'm not going to give up acting!"

"But a medical degree will make you a more interesting actor, and if acting jobs become scarce"—could they get more scarce? —"you'll have an equally rewarding second career."

His position shifted to not qualifying for premed studies and mine was that unless we looked into it, we'd never know. Over and over I pointed out that we had nothing to lose. "And there are all those fascinating things to learn." I admit that as the weeks passed I went from tearful begging to exploding with rage. We had gone through too damn many difficult years and I was insisting he give our family the chance it needed. I was unrelenting.

I had reached a point just short of murder when he agreed to look into it. All the news was good. Yes, he did qualify; yes, some prior college credits would even apply; and yes, a check for three hundred dollars would arrive each month!

So John went back to college and at last we had enough to pay the mortgage without borrowing from our families.

For the first time since we married, we could count on my husband to bring home the bacon *every* month. There was still premed and medical school, but we would make it now.

It was wonderful to see John's enthusiasm return as he became more and more fascinated by the wonders of science. There was an unending stream of interesting information to dispense. There were things I probably didn't really need to know, like how formaldehyde smelled on hands that had recently dissected a fetal pig. At nearly forty, John soon became dad to a group of young students who often came to our house to study. They all looked up to "Dad." His self-esteem soared.

After two years of study, John passed all premed exams with excellent grades and was ready for medical school. I wanted to tease Dodi into eating her words but we had lost touch for a while. I think she was out of the country at the time.

Medical schools are too few for the number of students who want to enter each year and age is a liability impossible to overcome. At forty-one, John was just too old to study in a place that could be filled by people with twice as many years to give to medicine. Unless he could isolate a virus or some similar discovery, he'd have to go to medical school in another country. We had no intention of giving up now, so John and I agreed that he would study medicine in Greece.

The house had to be sold. I convinced John that I didn't care. He promised to buy me a better one someday. A huge garage sale cleared the excess and the most-cherished of our hard-won treasures were carefully wrapped for storage in a watertight room. It would be at least four years, maybe more, before our return.

The final escrow papers were signed and five years of effort were gone. I secretly wept for the loss of my little house and for the life that never had a chance to be lived there. I took a private tour of all that we'd done. I memorized every detail, trying to imprint the images on a heart that would not forget. The struggle would be left way behind but the house would forever know.

Tears streamed into the keyboard and forced me to stop typing. The pain of losing the little house that had been home to my dreams was still in the depths of my being and erupting in sobs. I must have been carrying that pain for more than twenty years. Or were my tears washing over a lifetime of accumulated loss— loss that began early in childhood?

When the tears stopped, I felt proud to know that we had finished that house and found a way out. We hadn't given up.

I saved all my thoughts onto a reserve disk and closed the machine, confident that something significant was happening to me.

After dinner, I settled in to watch *Friends*. Jenny appeared and my thoughts were still full as I noticed traces of my little girl in that stunning young woman. I watched her familiar movements; I saw the grace there since she first learned to walk and her beauty so like my mother's. I kept thinking about Jen and my mother. Two women I loved intensely had chosen to separate their lives from mine. I decided to go digging in the ground from which I grew. Tomorrow.

But I waited a long time for sleep that night.

Chapter 6
A TANGLE
OF FEELINGS

THOUGHTS ABOUT MOTHER CONTINUED. My body tensed against the mattress as I recalled the shock when I learned that she wasn't going to live with us anymore. I had always regarded the way she left as cruel, but now I found myself wondering if a less brutal way would really have mattered. I wanted to sleep but my mind had more thinking to do.

For most of my early life I missed Mother and, without realizing it, I entered adulthood waiting for her to come back. Filled with those old feelings of longing, I fell into a fitful sleep.

Mother's voice, sweet and clear, was disturbing my sleep. "Go play now, dear." Fast moving trains, iron wheels against track, added to nightmarish dreams. I woke with a jolt, my heart pounding, my nightgown soaked with sweat, and grateful for morning. I slipped into a white cotton T-shirt and jeans.

Images of Mother persisted, which I interpreted as a clue to go deeper into that phase of my life. My confidence in the process of remembering as a potential for healing was growing. I knew it was time to dig deeper. Long-forgotten memories were opening doors that had closed eons ago, and it looked like Mother was trying to enter. I turned on my word processor.

When I was about seven, my parents crowded six kids and all of our belongings into an old Dodge sedan and drove from our home in New York to California. It seemed like that trip took forever. We had to behave and be quiet even though we four older girls were squeezed into the backseat and someone had Little Martha sitting on her lap. If we complained, Father said it's crowded in the front, too, with a new baby in the car bed between them. Father repeatedly said he was exhausted. Mother said the motion of the car made baby Sally sleep all day which is why she cried all night, and that kept Father from sleeping. Father said we should understand because he had to drive while the rest of us just sat there doing nothing. He was right about that. But it was really hard to just sit there doing nothing, so we couldn't help saying irritating things like, "When are we going to get there?" or "Why did we have to leave home anyway?"

Father was looking for a job, which was hard to find because many people were out of work in the Forties. If he didn't get one in California, we'd have to return home. I for one prayed that didn't happen, because I never wanted to take another trip like that again.

I was relieved when we found a little house and settled in California, but life didn't get any easier. Mother and Father seemed angry all the time. I can still hear him saying, "Get those gawdamned kids outta here!" Then Mother would say, "He's tired, go out and play." One time I overheard him ask, "Where the hell is that gawdamned kid?" I assumed that "gawdamned kid" was me so I decided to appear and make him happy. But he didn't seem happy when he snapped, "What are you doing in here?" It was scary to be caught in a dialogue with Father because I always said the wrong thing. "You wanted to know where the hell I was, so here I am."

The look on his face was fierce as he bellowed that I shouldn't use that word. He threatened to wash my mouth out with soap if I ever cursed again. He complained that kids shouldn't hang around the house all day. I resolved to try harder to remember which words were good and which weren't. I also tried to keep in mind that if Father wondered where I was, he probably meant something different. Mother said, "Try to remember, your father has two jobs and he's overworked and exhausted."

Mother never complained. She bore unbearable hardship, yet never complained.

I can't think about Mother without remembering how much I loved her. As I entered third grade in grammar school, the oblivion of childhood was being replaced by a heightened awareness of life. I would stand in the shadows just to watch her do chores, being quiet and unseen, or she'd send me outside to play. "Kids have no business in the house. Go outside and play now." I hated to see her work so hard but, held by the sight of her struggle, I couldn't stop watching. Her life was one backbreaking chore after another. It was well into the Forties but we still didn't have modern equipment like a washing machine, a vacuum cleaner, or an iron that plugged in. I'd watch her scrub clothes on a rippled metal board that was tilted in the sink, pausing only to rub the pain out of her hands. Then she'd lift soaking wet bed-sheets to wring a foot at a time as the water ran out. From that darkened corner I'd think, When I grow up I'm going to buy her a machine like the lady's next door.

One day Father told us that there was going to be a company picnic in the park and everyone had a chance to win a prize. Mother entered a race, and I cheered "Go Mommy" to help her win and was very excited when she did. They put her in a line to collect a prize and I stood next to her, hoping she'd get something nice. It was almost her turn when a man pushed his wife in front of Mother. That lady got a new iron with a cord, but with obvious disappointment she said, "I already have one!" Mother won a can of coffee. "We can always use coffee," she said. Father said that the woman in front of Mother was the boss's wife. I was mad for days and even madder when I saw Mother put that heavy black thing on the stove to heat so she could iron our clothes.

Mother had a beautiful smile though she didn't smile much or like to be hugged. I was sure that if her life hadn't been so hard, she would have been affectionate. I really wanted to hug her just once.

After Little Martha died, Mother took us east to stay with her parents while Father continued to work in Los Angeles until we got settled in a place of our own. But months passed without finding a place. Father did find a better job so we returned to California. After a while I heard arguments behind their bedroom door and pretty soon Mother took us east again, leaving Father behind.

We'd been living with our grandparents for nearly a year, but this time nobody was moving anywhere.

One morning I woke early. The snow had melted from the windowsill and birds were chirping the first sign of spring. Not wanting to wake my sister Linda, I slipped quietly out of bed. I was too excited to sleep. I had borrowed a bicycle and in a few hours two girlfriends would be pedaling over to join me for a long bike ride in the sun. It had been a cold, snowy winter and we planned to break out and enjoy the long-awaited spring warmth.

I dressed quickly and, leaving the room without waking my sister, I quietly tiptoed down the stairs that ended in a large front-entry room off the summer porch. I found Mother lying on the floor. My oldest sister, Joan, was heading upstairs as she said, "Mommy's been there all night." She had taken some pills to make her die but they didn't work. A doctor came in the middle of the night and had just left. Joan, at just fourteen, had been up all night watching people try to save our mother's life. She went upstairs to get some sleep. Grandmother came in and cautioned, "Now don't worry, she's going to be all right. She's just sleeping on the mattress from the sunporch lounge because no one was strong enough to carry her upstairs." Then with a scowl she said, "Your grandfather's really mad at her for doing this." Then Grandmother left the room.

I was too scared to be mad because Mother was mumbling, "I want to die." I sat on the floor watching her breathe and nearly stopped breathing myself.

"Mommy, don't die."

I didn't notice that Linda was downstairs until she said, "Don't be stupid, she's not going to die. Get some breakfast."

"No, she keeps trying to make herself stop breathing."

"That's stupid. She can't do that."

"I'm not leaving her alone."

I sat on the floor for a very long time to make sure she kept breathing. Later in the morning, Mother was sleeping peacefully, and I knew she was going to be all right.

When my friends arrived, I ran outside to greet them and right away we took off on our bikes. The sun was hot and for awhile I let them ride a short distance in front. The rays burned on my back, but I didn't notice because in my mind a secret was forming. If Mother cared about me she wouldn't want to die. She couldn't leave her kids if she loved us. The sun seemed to scorch that fact right into my brain but I vowed that no one would ever know. On the way back I called to my friends, "C'mon, let's race."

At home Mother was upstairs, sitting in bed, awake and talking. She said, "They told me you were worried and tried to help. Thank you, Dear."

"Shouldn't we go back to California?" I asked.

Things had a way of returning to normal. Grandmother was getting even more strict and she sighed more often than Mother. Grandmother wanted her house back and I wanted California. I began to put pressure on Mother to return to Los Angeles. One day Mother told us that arrangements were made and we'd be leaving for California soon. I was excited and became even more so when a big black trunk appeared in the upstairs hall near my bedroom door. Every day I'd open the lid to check on the packing progress, but each time the inside was as empty as ever. It seemed to loom larger and blacker and emptier with each lift. I'd ask, "Mommy, why haven't you started packing?" She'd always answer, "There's plenty of time."

It was odd how she said that, because one night she gathered the four of us older girls into the bedroom and said that we were scheduled to fly to California tomorrow. She and our youngest sister would not be going with us because the packing wasn't done and Sally was too young to travel alone. They would join us

90

in two weeks. I passed that trunk on the way to bed and for the last time lifted the lid. I noticed its cavernous insides had one white bed sheet neatly folded and placed on the bottom. I fell asleep wondering why Mother didn't have time to finish packing when I reminded her every day.

There were four small matching suitcases and we felt quite grown-up, each carrying our own, as we left for the airport. They let Mommy watch our departure out in the area next to the plane. I remember how small she looked standing down there as we took off.

Something didn't feel right and a few minutes into the flight I began to cry and call for my mother. Pretty soon a sailor sitting in front of me demanded that I shut up, but a devil was in me and I bawled even louder. My sister Jean told me we would see her in two weeks and that I should be quiet. But something was not letting up. I cried like that for another two hours until I, quite suddenly, vomited all over the place. In a flash the sailor disappeared and didn't return for more than an hour.

When the plane landed, Father said we looked pale. "Where's your mother and Sally?"

"They didn't come."

A terrible look came over Father's face and I wondered why Mother hadn't told him.

Father took us to a small hotel near where he worked. It wasn't a good place for kids so we soon moved into a two-bedroom apartment to wait for Mother and our little sister. Two weeks later, instead of herself and Sally, Mother sent a letter saying she wouldn't be coming—ever. Father's mouth twisted as he said that she was never coming back. He sat in the big gray chair with a piece of white paper dangling between two fingers and said terrible things about Mother. Sipping a scotch, he let go with his anger and we weren't permitted to leave. He was so upset that he failed to notice that I was in shock and suffering, too. I guess he thought we were too young to have feelings, and his were too out of control.

Father was deeply hurt, but in the days that followed I knew he still hoped she would return. When divorce papers arrived a few weeks later, his hurt turned to rage. There was no one to help ease his pain, and I'm sure even if there were, he wouldn't have known how to ask. So he drowned it in alcohol. For days he sat in the big gray chair just staring.

He came home late one night and while we slept, our dignified father vomited all over the front lawn of our building. He wore a sheepish grin in the morning when he asked my oldest sister to retrieve his teeth and eyeglasses from it. I felt sorry that she had to reach into that mess, but I was sure glad he hadn't asked me. Father was very embarrassed and for a while he cut down on the booze.

A tall, handsome man who walked with unusual grace for his height, Father's character was strong like the rocky terrain of Scotland where generations of our ancestors were born. His moodiness, worsened by Mother's departure, was as unyielding as Scotland's inclement weather. Chained to the dictates of his destiny, he moved irreconcilably away from his dreams. Father never did understand women, and raising four young daughters was, at times, more than a single man could handle. In his mind, the job of a parent was to criticize flaws such as foolish behavior and to guard a child from conceit by withholding praise. One day he took me aside to confide, in an offhand manner designed to hide any hint of praise, that my teacher told him to prepare me for college because my IQ was high and it would be a shame if I didn't further my education. When I told him I wanted to be an actress, he said, "That's foolish, everyone wants that. What makes you think you have a chance? Look, be smart, don't end up like me. Get a good education and marry a man who is well-situated, and always have dinner ready when he comes home."

It was true that Father's life wasn't great and some of what he said did make sense, so I shifted my dream to college.

Two times Father tried to wrest himself from the hindrance of dependent children and both times he failed. Late in the first year after Mother was gone, Father told us some unexpected news. "I heard about a home for girls who don't have mothers. They say it's a beautiful place and some nice women live there to take care of the girls. I have made an appointment for us to visit tomorrow." It sounded good to me because I was really missing my mother and there were so many things I couldn't tell Dad.

The next day, Father stayed home from work and we got to stay home from school. We bathed and made sure our hair was shiny clean. Above all, we promised we wouldn't giggle or act silly as we headed for what seemed destined to be our new home.

A nice woman opened the front door and I saw the glisten of high polish on the banister of a beautiful, winding staircase that emptied into a huge, tastefully decorated entry hall. On the far end an archway opened to a lovely main parlor that looked inviting. It was cozy and comfortable. I squinted my eyes for a better look at two girls in the distance. Would they be friendly?

Yes, this might be a nice place to live. But a few days later Father said, "No, you're going to stay here with me." He didn't tell us why and it wasn't our place to ask questions, because we were only kids. Soon the house and its beautiful furniture were forgotten and Father kept doing the best he could to give us the best he knew how.

One day I asked about his friend, "You know, that nigger from work?"

Father bellowed, "Don't ever say that word again!"

"Why?" I mentioned the names of some nice neighbors who said it, but father told me that only ignorant people use that word. He said it means that they think a whole race of people is not as good as they are. I was fiercely punished because Father said he didn't want me to ever forget.

My heart ached when Father said he'd worked hard all his life trying to save enough money to open a business so he could give us a better life. He said working for others is hell and he wished we could all pitch in and run some kind of business together. Poor Dad never found the money or the courage to make it happen, but did the best he could working for others.

Our small apartment came furnished but in pretty bad shape, which I boldly pointed out to the landlord. Father didn't like us to complain. If he found out there'd be hell to pay. Fortunately they never told him, but preferred to give us a better couch and some gray paint that matched Father's chair. I talked my oldest sister, Joan, into helping and together we painted the living room, which turned out quite well. It was definitely an improvement over the "mess" I'd made in our living room when I was five. Father just said we should thank God for what we had.

Father believed in helping the neighbors, though after working all day he really didn't have the energy. He'd force his large frame out of the chair to follow our disabled landlord to the latest clogged drain or flat tire. I wished just once he'd say no, but Father said it was only right.

94

Since we didn't have much money, Father believed that buying clothes was a terrible waste, so there was a constant battle over the few we had. The first one up got first pick and so on. One day I was the last to get dressed and there was only a torn slip and the dark blue corduroy coat left to wear. It was a hot day and my favorite teacher insisted that I remove the coat in his class. Of course I had to refuse.

He said, "You will or I'll call your mother!"

I said, "Go ahead, I don't have a mother."

His insistence waned and my "no" was the final word. On the way home from school, I agonized over the way I'd been forced to behave toward my favorite teacher. It would never happen again.

There was a dime store nearby and I had often wandered through the aisles to look at the beautiful things. That day I went to the clothes department and slipped a white angora sweater, a dark blue skirt, and a pair of socks into the large pockets of that coat. I walked out of the store with my heart pounding, legs trembling, and before reaching home I nearly fainted. Collapsing on my pillow I cried for an hour. I was only fourteen, but the next day I lied about my age and got a job in a movie theater near school. I'd already lost two jobs for confessing my real age, but this time I vowed not to divulge it to anyone.

As grown women, when talking with my sisters, we often marvel at how we survived in those years, taking care of each other. Joan could fix almost anything. If the sink got stopped up, she could open the pipe with a special tool and get the gunk out. Once she took the iron apart and made it work. But we needed a mom to talk to us when our periods started and to talk to about boys.

When we grew well into our teens (the twins were seventeen, I was fifteen, and Linda was thirteen), another plan was considered—the navy. Father decided to enlist all four of us girls in the navy. He said it would be a wonderful way to get a good education, important discipline, and three square meals a day. We could all retire young with a pension. I wasn't quite sure what a pension was, but it sounded good. Early one Sunday morning Father drove us to the recruiting office. Since there weren't many cars on the road, it didn't take long to get there so I didn't have much time to think it over, but that didn't really matter because the office was closed. Dad didn't say much as he turned the car around and headed home.

At work the next day someone told him that even with his permission Linda was too young to enlist. That ended that. If Linda couldn't go, none of us could, and he was damned if even the navy, with all its benefits, was going to separate us girls. He said we'd find out soon enough that we couldn't trust anyone but each other. Father never tired of telling us that we must always stick together because, as he said, "It's a tough world out there and your sisters are the only ones who won't let you down." He always added that he'd like to have a nickel for every damned so-called friend that let him down.

While Father never did quite manage to undo the tangle of his feelings, our grandfather had instilled a strong sense of duty that my father carried to his grave. A sense of duty still runs in his family to this day. Considering everything, my father did the best he could to raise four daughters who turned out to be good friends.

Our friendship, beyond sisterhood, didn't really take root until our teens when we began to share notes about romance and sex, each boasting that she knew more and sooner than the others. Some big points were scored by one of the twins when she confided that there were condoms buried under some papers in a hatbox on the top shelf of Father's closet. We had endless giggles speculating about what our old dad might be doing with them and feeling quite grown-up that we knew full well the implications of our discovery. It did seem as if he was in a better mood. Later I went to have a look for myself and found the papers in the box quite intriguing. I opened an envelope that contained the divorce papers Mother had sent and was shocked to the core by my discovery. When it asked for the number of children someone had typed in "ONE." One, named Sarah Mae Dow. Sally? I stood on the chair, my eyes glued to that paper. No Nancy? Was I less than unloved? Was I never born? The information sank into the dark corner of my being where the secret about Mother's suicide attempt lay.

I was seventeen and it was almost time for me to graduate from high school. I was excited about going away to college. Father seemed surprised when I asked where I would go. I was surprised when he said there wasn't enough money, and that I had to keep working. So I applied for a better job at a movie studio. My work there seemed to rekindle another old dream. Not long after that, Father announced that he would marry a woman he'd been dating and that I and my two older sisters would have to find a place of our own. Life without Father would definitely be more peaceful. It was the Fifties, when people still felt safe enough to leave their doors unlocked, but for me, I felt alone and scared.

At just seventeen, starved for affection and too scared to be alone, I soon met a man and decided to marry. He was a good man from a wonderful family. Just what I wanted, he was an older man who seemed to promise what a frightened teenage girl needed. But it turned out that with such deep-rooted insecurity I simply couldn't be married, especially to a man I found incapable of expressing the affection that had been lacking. The child who longed to be hugged felt she had married a man who was hugless.

By the time I became pregnant, it was pretty clear that I'd chosen the wrong man. I had been much too young and needy to have taken such an important step. Having borne the pain of losing a parent, it was hard to risk the same for my son, yet when he was only two and a half I sued for a divorce.

I stopped typing to mull over the flood of memories I'd been absorbing for days. It was beginning to appear that this review may have revealed the cause of my most difficult flaws: the tendency to be a chronic worrier. I could see that the loss of Little Martha, followed by Mother's departure, and then my own divorce at such a young age made it hard to trust in the "outcome."

I was wondering what to do with this news when a second revelation began to dawn. Those two trips to stay with our grandparents had probably been failed attempts by Mother to leave Father! But it was impossible for a divorced woman to survive with five children in those days. At once Mother's choice seemed limited to me: suicide or send us to live with Father. I squeezed the tension from my shoulders with both hands. I could imagine Mother spending agonizing hours trying to think of ways to keep us as she dealt with the pain of realizing that the only solution was to leave her children. It was a startling revelation that somehow conveyed a sense that Mother did love me!

I went outside to walk in the garment of Mother's love, trying it on for size. It had the lovely feeling of silk that was sized to fit and moved well.

98

Another day had been spent discovering that feelings, long forgotten, were still there. As the effort brought clarity to the past, the present was becoming clearer. Something important was taking place. There's a valuable person here and it just might be me.

I sank into a big chair and recalled that it had taken years before I stopped missing Mother. I was struck by the irony of my own daughter not wanting hers. Yet this separation from Jen was beginning to make sense.

Sitting in the fading light, I allowed myself to brood that I still hadn't heard from Johnny or Jen. As I often did, I took a mental inventory of who needed me. It was strange to find there was no one to worry about. For the first time ever I felt like nobody's anything.

I remembered that morning after Jen's declaration to "never forgive me" and how that second caller had nearly pushed me over the edge. During sessions at church it had surfaced that the abuse in that call wasn't the first time I'd taken such a bruising, and we diagnosed a weakness in me that allowed it to happen.

It might be that inordinate fear of loss had contributed to my willingness to tolerate less acceptable behavior and was also a manifestation of weakness. On some level, those who loved me may have recognized the weakness and it was pushing them away. No one, of any age, wants to see that in a person, especially a parent.

I surrendered myself to these thoughts. Pain, joy, doubt, and fear had all lived in epic proportions within, waiting unnoticed, to be activated by the changing conditions of my life. The past clashing with the present had predetermined my future. I'd been a prisoner for years.

It was time to break out.

Chapter 7

HOPES AND DREAMS ABROAD

I T WASN'T SO EASY. STUMBLING blocks got in the way. As I described to a friend, reliving the past is like a room that's left empty when a young person leaves home for college. The child matures, and then comes back to the room to find that everything is still the same, yet somehow quite different. Of course, the perspective has changed. When I reviewed my childhood from the perspective of age, new light had been cast on the deeds of my parents. It was taking time to absorb the full impact of accepting Mother's love. After years of doubt I was dazed.

A battle was waging inside of me. In one counseling session I might be defiant: "No, I'm not like that," then in another I would acquiesce: "Sometimes it's hard to hear the truth." I replayed the tape of that fateful tabloid interview for my friends, asking, "What is so terrible?"

Everyone seemed to agree. "Nothing. Jennifer wants to be free."

"Of me?"

Life without contact with my kids meant living with death every day. I struggled to harmonize my feelings with all that was taking place. Incessant worry put knots in the pit of my stomach. Was Jen driving too fast, coming home late by herself, or skipping meals? Were Johnny and and his wife, Shannon, still excited to be expecting a baby so soon after their wedding? Was Shannie taking good care of herself and eating well for the baby? *Would I ever see my grandchild?*

I wanted to write in my journal but my thoughts were chained to the present.

Reverend Jim had said, "The only one we're permitted to change is ourselves." Being a chronic worrier was my problem, but I didn't know how to change. A veil seemed to be lifting as flaws in my nature appeared. When my daughter was old enough to take care of herself, had I spoiled her passage into adulthood with too many warnings of danger? I hadn't worried as much about Johnny, but he was a strong, healthy man. It looked like I had not only failed as a mother, but I was a closet sexist, too. Days passed into weeks as I wandered through a labyrinth of self-doubt and shame.

One day, I woke to an experience that mercifully shifted my train of thought. As I lay in bed, taking in the morning, I had a strong feeling that something was different but didn't know what. A careful search of my psyche revealed that this strange sensation was the absence of fear! Some kind of opening in me had cleared and peace was moving in. I knew in that brief moment I hadn't lived a day of my life without fear. I held very still, not wanting to move lest it change. Wonderful, glorious peace. I hoped it would last forever.

The implications were vast. What had I done or left undone due to fear? I felt a strong urge to dig deeper. My journal invited me to go exploring again. When I began typing, memories poured in like water from a broken faucet. I was once again back in the summer of 1974, a time when years of struggle in California had just ended.

Signing escrow papers and the exchange of money transferred the house, and five years of hard work, to another family. It was time for us to move in the direction of the country where John lived as a baby, until his parents immigrated with their young family to America. We planned to stay in a suburb of Philadelphia with Yaya for a while before crossing the Atlantic, which meant returning to the area where I might reunite with the mother I'd lost as a child.

It made sense to stay with John's mother until the University of Athens opened for classes. For the first leg of our long journey, we decided to travel by train. Four brand-new passports, waiting to boast exotic stamps from places that only lived in our dreams, and four open plane tickets to Athens were carefully stashed in a safe place. We were going east to wait for the future to give birth to expectations that were bursting our seams.

"I hope you can locate your mother," Molly said with encouragement. She tried to hide her tears as we held each other for what might be the last time in years. I promised to write when there was news. We loaded a big black trunk, similar to the one Mother failed to pack so many years ago, and one suitcase each into my sister Linda's family car. Her husband joined our excitement as they chauffeured us to the train station.

On the way we admired our decision to take the train. It would be a rare opportunity to see the country we were leaving, and if it turned out that we liked living in Greece, we might not return to America for a very long time. We wanted our kids to leave their country with its grand size and varied terrain imprinted on their minds.

Wanting to conserve the money from the sale of our house, we opted to forego a sleeping compartment. The money had to last through years of study in Greece. We reasoned that four seats facing each other would create our own private little area while we gazed out the windows, absorbing the wonders of our magnificent country. Reality failed to meet our expectations. The only four seats facing each other were taken by a family with a crying baby, and the windows were so cloudy from neglect that we couldn't see out. It became more and more impossible to sleep in train seats and by the end of five days, our enthusiasm for the trip had changed to frequent inquiries about when it would ever end. We arrived at the train station in Philadelphia looking like rejects from a secondhand store.

Our imaginations remained filled with sugarplum visions of a new life in the land of John's birth. Nothing could get us down. After a shower, a fantastic meal, and a sound sleep in proper beds, we bounced right back. The kids and I adored John's large, close-knit family who never tired of our questions about life in Greece. Weeks passed and I languished in the warmth of their love as we all got to know each other. Yaya insisted that John and I have her bedroom while she bunked with Jennifer in the room where her daughters had grown into women. Little Johnny settled in Big John's old room and was fascinated by things "Dad" had left there since childhood. We loved Yaya's stories about growing up on the island of Crete.

I interrupted my typing to savor those days and recalled how well we all managed to live together. I was reminded of the dream I'd had as a child to have a close family of my own one day, and I decided in that moment that those years with John's family were the best my dream could offer.

Eventually it grew hard to contain our eagerness to go to Greece. Political unrest between Cyprus and Turkey caused a crisis in Greece and the University of Athens remained closed long after the summer break ended. It was late September, well past the date when most universities begin classes. Waiting became intolerable. John decided to go on alone. I didn't mind because it allowed more time to practice the Greek alphabet and to memorize more words. I wanted to communicate with those faces I'd seen in Yaya's photo album.

I'd been thinking about my mother and decided I would try to locate her while we were waiting. As that eastbound train ate up miles of rail, bringing me nearer to where she lived, my wish to see her increased. I leaned back, wresting my attention from the word processor and realized for the first time that, though it didn't seem so long ago, she had probably been about the same age as I was. How quickly a lifetime passes.

Yaya was happy when I discovered that my mother was living in the neighboring state of Connecticut. She urged me to make contact. It took several days to find the courage to call. What if she rejected me again? I knew I had to take that chance, but I stared at the telephone number for a couple of days before finding the courage to dial. I nearly wept when my call made her happy. Mother wanted to meet my two children, so we planned to visit the following week. The six-year-old sister I hadn't seen for twenty-five years lived nearby and invited me and the kids to stay with her. I

105

was delighted. Sally was a stranger by now and spending that much time together would give us a chance to really connect.

There was an instant recognition with Sally. We didn't stop talking for nearly two days. But the visit with Mother turned out to be a short lunch in a neighborhood restaurant.

Mother was smaller than I remembered. Her full crop of dark, curly hair was cut short and colored reddish brown. The sparkle in her deep-blue eyes had dimmed and her face was an ominous gray, but she had the same beautiful smile I often see in my own children. She had recently undergone a radical mastectomy because a hard lump in her breast was found to be malignant. Mother still wasn't feeling very well. When the short lunch was over, her turkey sandwich had only one bite missing. She hugged the children, and I hoped she'd feel better soon. As we got into the car, I could see in the mirror that she waved until we drove out of sight.

It was already November, and although the political situation in Greece had somewhat eased, the university was still closed. John said he didn't like being without us. "It's better if we get to know Greece together. You can learn the language even quicker. Please, come soon."

Greece was an exciting adventure for the whole family. We stayed in Athens with John's sister and her fourteen-year-old son who was Johnny's age. Quick to become buddies, together they ganged up on Jen, a typical little girl who both loved and hated it.

John and I learned something about children and about communicating. Jennifer would spend hours in conversation with the concierge of our building speaking only English while the older lady spoke only Greek. Neither seemed to notice that each used a language the other didn't understand and passed many afternoons chatting away. We all agreed that in a few more months Jennifer would be fluent in Greek.

The university finally opened and endless hours were spent trying to convince administrators that John needed to enroll. When red tape strangled every option, outside help was enlisted, yet despite the valiant efforts of a great many people, no one could get the desired results. Due to a military incursion from Turkey, the university in Cyprus had been closed and all nine thousand Cypriot students were given a transfer to the University of Athens. There wouldn't be room to admit any foreign students that year! Relatives with clout arranged numerous appointments with high-ranking government officials, but it was like changing the tide.

We feared it was hopeless, but some of our relatives were determined that our trip was not to be in vain. They kept trying. In the meantime, we decided that nothing was going to spoil our love of Greece. I had been doing the cooking chores and loved shopping at the outdoor street market where the farmers came to sell their freshly picked produce. I learned to prepare some Greek dishes that everyone said were delicious. With fresh vegetables and Greek olive oil, it was hard to go wrong. We even found a group at the American Military Club who played bridge.

It was soon Christmas and 1975 arrived with the usual celebrations all over the city. In Greek tradition, we played games to see who would have good luck in the following year. John was the big winner. Jennifer had her sixth birthday in February and John was still trying to hack through red tape. One day we got the final word that there was nothing more to be done. All hope was gone. John was officially and most definitely denied the opportunity to study medicine in Greece. His sister suggested that we spend a few weeks sight-seeing before returning home to the States. With our future once again uncertain, we were forced to see Greece on a shoestring budget. Regardless, everything and everyone everywhere was enchanting.

We took a boat to Crete and docked near the ancient city of Knossos. We wandered through the maze where Theseus slew the Minotaur and saved the day for ancient Greece. We visited the town where John was born and the large farm where Yaya was raised. Yaya's youngest brother and his family still lived in that timeless setting, with several relatives nearby who were eager to meet family from America. It was a large farm with acres of olive trees and grapevines used to make Uncle Theo's wine. As we walked through ancestral villages, Yaya's stories came alive.

Jennifer met cousins her age and had a wonderful time playing games. A large field near Theo's house was covered by lush green plants with little yellow flowers they call "horta." The girls went with the aunts to pick armloads for dinner and all the women formed a circle in the large kitchen to prepare them for cooking. A portion of the horta was chopped with onion and stuffed into their filo pastry dough for sumptuous hors d'oeuvres and the rest was boiled as a vegetable side dish with dinner. During the meal, a funny story was recounted by Aunt Thea. She told of chasing a headless chicken around the yard as it stubbornly refused to become our main course. I would have enjoyed the chicken more if I hadn't heard the details of its recent demise, but it's their custom to have fresh meat for meals. I filled up on horta. And more horta! Those greens with their little yellow flowers were delicious. I couldn't stop eating them.

That night a volcano was brewing in my stomach and exploded in epic proportions. It was extremely fortunate that

108

they had an American toilet because the customary hole cut into the floor, found in less modern buildings, would have been a disaster. The bathroom adjoined Aunt Thea and Uncle Theo's bedroom, but I was the only one using it that night. In the morning everyone asked how I was feeling as they exchanged knowing glances, saying, "It's the horta."

After returning to Athens, John's sister generously offered her van for a wonderful tour of southern Greece. We feasted on cheese, olives, and Theo's wine, and listened to traditional Greek music while three-thousand-year-old ruins became commonplace. John told us that the enchanting sound coming from our radio and filling the car for miles with its unusual lilt was a Greek-style guitar called a bouzouki. As we rounded one bend, line dancers in native costumes appeared out of nowhere while the expanse of their ancient land glistened like gold in the sun. The magic of Greece captured our hearts. John said we would enjoy our next visit even more when our finances improved and our lives were on solid ground.

In early spring, with no plans for the future, we decided it was time to return to the States. With that decision, another nightmare began.

At that time, the Greek government required that all Greek-born men serve in the military, and John's citizenship had never been revoked. John was in the odd position of being on the one hand considered a citizen for military purposes, but on the other a foreign student when it came to his eligibility for study at the university. The men who held positions of authority appreciated the peculiar dichotomy, but with the amused certainty of those in charge they expressed that John should want to do his patriotic duty. They refused to permit him to leave the country until a two-year stint in the army had been completed! A second wave of phone calls and visits to officials followed but things weren't looking good. Everyone understood our need to get home, but to the Greek officials surely a *man* would *want* to serve his country. It seemed like a miracle when a technicality, the nature of which none of us understood, was discovered that allowed John to receive the requisite stamp on his passport. We were finally allowed to leave the country.

We lost no time packing our things and heading off for the airport, but not before receiving a grim warning that at any moment, until the cabin door closed and the plane was in the air, John could be detained by any zealot in a uniform. I climbed the stairs to the fuselage on legs that felt like rubber. As the plane broke through the clouds and into blue sky, I shed tears of sadness for the loss of a dream, while my heart sang with joy for the deliverance.

When we arrived at Yaya's house near Philadelphia, Jen still wasn't fluent in Greek and I continued having problems from the horta. We arrived in the States homeless. Yaya offered to put us up while we planned our next move. We gratefully accepted. At one point John remembered that the school for Homeopathic Medicine was in the area and perhaps he might be accepted for study next semester. Few people want to practice homeopathics because its natural-healing remedies are more difficult to dispense than the common-variety drugs and may bring fewer financial rewards. Visions of a more lucrative practice lure most young students away, which results in a lighter demand for study. As supporters of homeopathy, the prospects, for us, looked promising.

Perhaps as a buffer against disappointment, I began thinking that it really wouldn't matter if medical school didn't happen at

110

all. The main thing had been to get John's energy moving and to bring vitality to a career that had completely run out of steam. I was beginning to notice that the obstacles we had overcome during the last few months may have wrought many changes in John, and a different actor was emerging from the experience. The ordeal itself had set something in motion and I was sure that a remarkable confidence had been awakened in John's whole manner. The purpose had always been to make a move—any move—that would end his lethargy. Something was gaining momentum and it looked like my strategy had worked. I really did hope something positive was about to happen because we had all sacrificed so much. It would have been a tragedy for nothing to come of it.

In the meantime, I enrolled the kids in local public schools near Yaya's house and tried to create a normal life. I worried that Jennifer might have a difficult time adjusting to a school so different from the one she'd known. But kids are resilient and despite all the moving around, she was one six-year-old who could fit right in. Johnny easily adjusted to his new school.

John decided it might help our finances if he spent a day in Manhattan connecting with some old friends in the business. He would try to get some acting work while waiting to apply to medical school.

When he made that trip to New York City, Yaya and I lit a candle and said a silent prayer.

He returned home with good news. An old friend, an agent, thought John looked fantastic and said, "You've got the perfect look for a part I'm trying to cast." The agent sent him right over to audition for a daytime series. A few days later they called back for more talks and a screen test. When John phoned with the news that he was signed for the part of Edward Aleata on *Love of Live*, Yaya and I stood in her tiny kitchen, held onto each other, and cried.

It took a New Yorker to appreciate the "look" we'd created in California. Years of struggle had finally paid off. The battle to get John to fight for his career had ended. I felt as if my husband had recovered from a long illness, a kind of paralysis. I wanted to shout it from the rooftops and say to my friend Dodi, "Thank God I stood by my man." Our family was intact and everything was going to be all right. Joy filled my entire being! New York City was going to be our next hometown. The future lay before us like Christmas morning with its carefully wrapped gifts waiting to reveal their surprises.

John commuted from Yaya's for a time to adjust to the job, while the kids finished out the semester in school. I wanted to share my good news with Mother. She was happy for us but didn't feel well enough to stay on the phone. By midsummer we had found a three-bedroom apartment, a rarity in Manhattan, in a very tall building with a spectacular view of downtown. It was time to move to the big city. We packed our clothes, borrowed a couple of beds from Yaya, and took off to live the dream we had held for so long.

My father, Gordon McLean Dow.

My mother, Louise Grieco Dow.

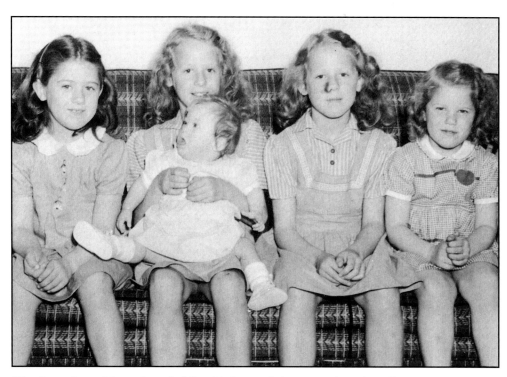

The Dow sisters: Nancy, Jean (holding Little Martha), Joan, and Linda (Sally was not born yet).

Professional pictures taken of me in the mid to late 1960s.

John Aniston and I (1965). It was a small wedding and a simple dress, but dreams about our future, vows about forever, and love filled my heart.

Baby Jenny, one and a half weeks old, with her mom (1969).

Johnny proudly holds his new baby sister (1969).

Johnny always seemed to wrap brotherly love around his little sister (1971).

While playing in the park in the hot California sun, a protective brother makes sure Jenny has drinks of cool water (1971).

Jenny's baptism celebration at the Savalas house following the ceremony; Penelope, Telly, me holding Jen, John, and Lynn Savalas (1971).

Penelope here looks after her newly christened godsister (1971).

Jenny sits alone in a log cabin playhouse, waiting for the older kids to come down from Johnny's treehouse to play with her (1972).

Lynn and I often took the kids to Griffith Park, Los Angeles. Here, in 1972, Jenny, Penelope, and Candace wait for a turn on the merry-go-round.

Christmas with the Savalases: Johnny, Jenny, Lynn, me, and Telly (1972).

A portrait of our girls: Candace, Jenny, and Penelope (1972).

We shared many lovely Christmas holidays at the Savalas house.

My favorite picture of Jenny, wearing an adorable outfit that Lynn bought her for Christmas.

Jenny adored her Yaya (grandmother; 1974).

It surprised and delighted us to find that my camera had captured Jenny and her dad with the same pouty expression (1974).

Jenny telling a story to her class at the little nursery school I helped start in our church (1974).

Johnny, Jen, and me relaxing for a minute as we climbed the ruins at Knossos on the island of Crete in Greece (1975).

My son took this picture of us.

Jen and Johnny leaving an old building in downtown Athens (1976).

John and I at our first gala event for *Love of Life* (1977).

Jenny and I at Kennedy Airport in New York City before boarding the plane for a summer visit with Johnny in California (1979).

Molly, Jen, cousin Kimberly, and me. An outing with Molly was always a special treat for us (1979).

Jen and I at the front door of Johnny's apartment (1980).

Some friends invited Jen and me to spend the afternoon cruising the Pacific Ocean on their boat (1980).

Here we are celebrating my summer birthday in California at the home of Molly and Bill Reynolds (1980).

Jen wearing her brother's Dallas Cowboy jersey the summer he took her to watch the team at spring training camp (1981).

Johnny and his sister always had such fun being silly together (1981).

Johnny and I in his apartment with the "repaired" guitar in the background (1982).

Me, Jean, Jen, and Joan. Jenny enjoyed sitting with us around Aunt Joan's kitchen table as we reminisced about our childhood (1982).

The Aniston girls and Molly share a laugh together at my birthday party on Aunt Joan and Uncle Don's patio (1983).

Dinner with the Reynolds: Eric Reynolds, me, Jen, Johnny, Molly, and Bill Reynolds (1985). Bill played Agent Colby on the long-running television show *The FBI*.

A family gathering at Aunt Linda and Uncle Al's home (1991). This was the first time all five Dow girls (seated in the front row) were together since being separated as children.

Portfolio shots I took of Jennifer in the early stages of her career (mid to late 1980s).

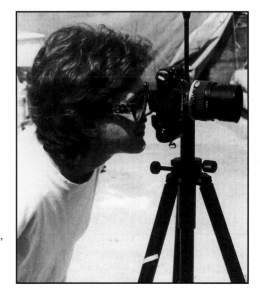

I still enjoy taking photos (photo by Coral Leigh, 1992).

Our first Christmas together after I moved back to California in 1991.

It was wonderful for the three of us to be living close enough to celebrate the holidays together.

Christmas dinner at my house.

Me, Jen, Johnny, and his new wife, Shannon, at the wedding reception for the bride and groom shortly after they returned from their honeymoon in Greece (1995).

Jennifer and I, watching the caterers set up before the guests arrive for the reception.

Linda, Jennifer, Jean, and me, delighted that Johnny chose such a lovely girl to add to our family.

Christmas 1995.

Jennifer and Shannon exchanging gifts on Christmas day, 1995.

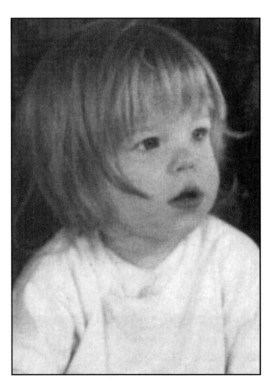

Johnny and Shannon's baby girl, my most splendid joy, my granddaughter (1998).

Chapter 8

SETTLING INTO THE UPPER WEST SIDE

I T WAS JUST A YEAR since our family had left California and headed east to bask in the promise of medical school. So much had happened. With Greece still fresh on our minds, we arrived in New York City to catch a dream we had almost abandoned. With overwhelming feelings of gratitude and excitement, I introduced my children to a whole new way of life. Because of a lifelong fear of heights, I was stunned to find that we would be living on the twenty-first floor of a high-rise building. Helping me overcome that fear was a view of downtown Manhattan, unobstructed all the way from our upper-west-side home to the water at the tip of Battery Park.

Everyone warned us against muggers, so Johnny taught me how to make a weapon with my keys. He placed one key between each finger of my fist and said one good punch with that and a mugger is history. I preferred to keep looking over my shoulder and Jennifer went on trusting everyone.

There was the fortunate news that the Rudolf Steiner School, a nearby private school, taught the Waldorf method. After years of struggle to get Johnny through a public system that never seemed to understand or appreciate his inquisitive mind, or was able to channel his abundant energy or cope with a child who was too advanced, I was grateful that one of our children would be able to attend a school that considered education an art and each child unique.

A short drive across Central Park and Jennifer would have the advantage of an educational philosophy that introduces intellectual concepts artistically and in a way that educates feeling while at the same time keeps the whole child in balance. I had observed that many of us are forced to contend with overdeveloped feelings while others struggle with an imbalance in thinking. This school might give Jen a better start in life.

Johnny refused to attend that "weird" school. For him weird meant no sports program like they have in the public schools he was used to. So, I was forced to enroll him in P.S. 86, a very good public school down the street. For the first time in his fifteen years Johnny had excellent teachers. He thrived.

As exciting as it was to live in New York City, it took some getting used to. One day, Jennifer and I arrived home at our bus stop and as the driver pulled up to the curb, there was a drunk sleeping it off on the sidewalk right in front of the door to the bus. We found it nearly impossible to step off the stairs and over the sprawling body. Breathing his rancid scent was also an unpleasant experience. As we walked away, Jennifer held my hand but continued looking back in amazement at the man lying on

114

the sidewalk. We took a few steps in silence as I searched for the right words to explain the encounter. Then Jen looked up with a serious face and asked if I thought the man had wanted to be that when he was little. I said, "Probably not." She then wondered if Daddy and Johnny would ever do that. Jennifer had her first dose of a reality quite unheard of in the suburbs of southern California, and found many interested ears in school the next day. The experience soon became part of our everyday life.

Another adjustment was needed to learn how to walk down the street with so many people moving at a speed-walker's pace. My first try was a disaster. It was beginning to be winter and I decided to get an early start on my Christmas shopping. The bus on our corner went right to the entrance of Macy's. It couldn't have been more convenient. I hopped on, feeling silly for not having done it sooner. But when I exited at the corner of Macy's, I stepped right into a wall of people. It was the largest crowd I'd ever seen moving that fast on a sidewalk. Every time I attempted to take a step a body was there to prevent it. I tried for several minutes before I turned around, crossed the street, and took the next uptown bus home. I soon learned that a short drive up the Henry Hudson Parkway and over the George Washington Bridge left the crowds and the tempo behind. This California girl found New Jersey Malls and vowed to become a New York shopper—later.

The next opportunity to experience the city came when the newspaper announced that it was time for the ice-skating show and the yearly lighting of a giant Christmas tree in Rockefeller Center. Johnny spent most of the time in his bedroom trying to escape raging hormones with the Moody Blues. He removed the headphones long enough to say that he wasn't interested in seeing tree lights go on, and Big John was too busy to go.

Undaunted by the threat of muggers, I decided to take Jennifer by myself. We arrived early to get an unobstructed view and held fast to our spot by the railing. On that cold, winter day, we stood under a patch of blue sky that peeked out at the top of the tallest buildings we'd ever seen. We watched our breath and waited for the ice-skating to begin. The orchestra was playing the overture when it became obvious that a California shoulder doesn't stand a chance against a New York elbow. A group of young people elbowed their way into our spot and completely blocked my little six-year-old's view. Jennifer started to cry and I tried to reason with them. It was a heartwarming surprise to find that a group of streetwise New York teenagers understood that the West Coast was a long way from the event they had seen many times. They not only cleared out a spot next to the rail, but also made a protective circle to keep other invaders away and cautioned us to be careful in the future. When the ice-skaters appeared, we were dazzled by the beauty of their shimmering costumes and graceful movements as they glided in rhythm to a whole array of musical numbers. With great authority, the young people explained everything before it happened.

Then the sun went down. We discovered that in the east, when the winter sun sets, the temperature drops fast. Coats that served well in the Sunshine State just didn't cut it against the bitter cold, and in no time we were freezing. But Jennifer wouldn't hear of leaving, so we toughed it out.

To conclude the show, millions of colored lights were turned on to light the biggest tree we'd ever seen. It was a spectacular sight. In an instant an enormous crowd of people filled the streets and sidewalks. Our protectors had vanished and I couldn't penetrate that mob, which in no time filled every available cab. We made our way to the nearest bus and virtually trembled with cold. Each step became more biting. Little Jenny began to sob. I guided her into the lobby of every other building to get warm, then we braced ourselves for another few yards. We limped along that way for blocks until we squeezed ourselves onto an overcrowded, overheated bus. The warmth from all those bodies was sheer ecstasy.

In the years to follow we preferred to watch this event on television, but I never forgot those helpful kids. To find friendliness in that unlikely group gave me confidence and respect for New York that was reinforced many times in the years to come. At last I began to feel at home in the world's tallest city.

Most days passed without incident and gradually, New York City became less and less menacing.

Meanwhile, I had called my mother in Connecticut several times, but she wasn't feeling well enough for a second visit. I still had questions to ask and years of catching up to do, so I kept calling. One time her husband answered the phone. He said she was in the hospital and if I wanted to see her, I should come soon. I arranged to stay with my sister Sally again and I was on a train to Hartford the next day. At last we would have that good talk.

By the time I arrived at the hospital, there wasn't much to visit except the worst pain I had ever seen. There aren't words to describe her suffering. There lay this little woman hanging onto the last of her dwindling life, deep-breathing and softly saying, "Oh dear, dear, dear" and "Oh my, my, my." I didn't think it was possible for a human being to bear that much pain with so much dignity. Once, and only once, I heard her say, "It's a mighty big price, a mighty big price."

Cancer was giving her a terrible beating, yet she was taking it like a trooper. Despite the years of people saying she didn't deserve to have children, I loved her deeply. Now I understood why. For ten days Sally dropped me off on her way to work in the morning, then came after dinner when visiting hours were over to take me to her home. Day after day I sat by Mother's bed trying to make up for lost time in a world of morphine and pain. Though she contributed very little, in the end we had shared something quite special.

It was getting close to our first Christmas in New York and I needed to get home to my family. When I told her I had to leave, she grabbed my hand and pleaded with me not to go. I couldn't believe that the mother who had resisted my visit for months and my presence in her life for most of mine, wanted desperately for me to stay. I promised to return right after the holiday and leaned over to kiss her good-bye. Not only was it the first kiss we'd ever exchanged but I also heard her softly say, "I love you, Nanny"— the words I had waited a lifetime to hear.

The day after Christmas the telephone rang. It was my sister Sally. "Mommy died today." I lowered the phone, walked quietly to the window, and gazed unseeing at the city lights, thinking, "She never came back." It was a most peculiar thought. Could it be that a grown woman, with kids of her own, was still waiting for her mother to come back?

The last thing I remember about my mother was driving away, in that long black car, as they lowered her casket into the snow-covered ground. I noticed a large wreath of white roses with a banner that read, "Good-bye, Mommy."

Good-bye, Mommy.

Chapter 9
CHOICES

T HE GENEROUS HAND OF DESTINY allowed me to share Mother's final days. A longing I had carried with me since childhood was now gone. Her death brought closure, and added emphasis to all the other changes in my life. It seemed a sure sign that a long and difficult period had ended.

There was a lot to think about on the train ride home from Mother's funeral. A room full of tall men in overcoats had stood near her casket and openly wept as they prayed. I learned that after she left us and Father, that brilliant mind had carried her through a series of jobs, climbing the corporate ladder to become a vice president in a large company that was run primarily by males. Several expressed admiration for this "special lady" and told stories of how she had helped them with problems, whether at work or at home. Apparently Mother was a kind humanitarian who never failed to go to bat for a coworker in need. What a strange dichotomy: she hadn't been there for her children, but she couldn't do enough to help others. Who was this woman in their stories?

The rhythm of the wheels droned on in the background as the sadness of Mother's death met prospects for the future in a steady stream of thoughts about the past. "It's a mighty big price" played out in the rhythm of the rail. Had it been Mother's way of saying I'm sorry?

After so many years without her, it had seemed right not to tell my sisters in Los Angeles, but now I was sorry that they hadn't been there. I tried to comfort myself with the knowledge that Mother had to leave us because she and Father didn't know how to love each other or their children. They had inherited this lack from their own families and remaining together as a couple would not have overcome it. Both had been prisoners of anger, frustration, and unhappiness worsened by poverty. I wondered if the element she had fled in her marriage had been the lack of interest, understanding, and kindness. As the train neared Manhattan, I gained strength from the fact that in my family, with the two children and the husband who were waiting for me, there was always an abundance of supportive interest in each other. And we had laughter. Mother hadn't had much of that and I hoped she had found a good life with that stranger I met in the hospital. The train was nearing home.

In one of our brief exchanges on the telephone, Mother confessed to years of nightmares about our safety. Then why hadn't she called? What had her life been like? Other than turkey sandwiches, what did she eat? And her friends—were they nice? Did she have many? My questions would remain unanswered forever. I wept for the final loss of my mother.

In a moment of perverse reason, I wondered if Mother had made a sacrifice to live without her children in order to give me the strength to keep my family intact during tough times. I shuddered to think of life without Jennifer and Johnny.

There was a warm, enthusiastic greeting waiting when I arrived home. Jennifer, in her child's need to understand everything, asked why she had been too young to go with me. She had never seen anyone dead and wanted to know what Grandmother looked like. Little Johnny and Big John showed concern and offered sympathy. But we had all been through enough for too many years and I didn't want to be the cause of any more grief. I said I was fine and preferred to be distracted by the tasks that lay ahead. We had been living in Manhattan for more than six months and there was still a lot of settling in to do.

In the early days of our marriage, we decided that John would handle our finances. I signed over all of my checks to his charge. Now that he was busy with work I offered to take over the job, but he preferred to keep things as they were, insisting that he better understood the process of paying our bills. He calculated that it was too costly to move our things from storage in California to New York and said that with the high cost of living in Manhattan, we had to continue to limit our spending. So I once again furnished a complete house on a tight budget. With everyone still needing clothes, careful budgeting really was necessary and neither of us wanted to fall into debt.

From the beginning, no matter how short the money, I fiercely opposed going into debt. I didn't want to mortgage our future to buy our way out of the reality we'd created. It also kept hope alive. Living within our means guaranteed that when John earned a dependable income, it wouldn't be absorbed by payments for things we had long ago discarded. It had become second nature to buy only what was absolutely necessary. I was willing to continue that policy because I believed that to live with dignity and grace was more rewarding than to live the insatiable existence of purchase and discard that is so prevalent today. The stress of managing on a grossly insufficient income was gone and budgeting was much easier now. My family was intact and that was the most important thing. As far as the money and its management, I was exhausted from years of moving a mountain and had little resistance left. I was perfectly content to handle the work of everyday life and let John make the decisions.

In the months to come, I watched John fall right into the role of the successful actor he is today. I wondered what had prevented him from functioning fully for so many years. I had no regrets because I gained a sound feeling of security knowing that my family was resting on the solid foundation of John's appreciation for having survived hard times together. For the first time ever I felt confidence in life. But I did come to realize that I had been carrying too much responsibility for someone else's life. I vowed that I would never do it again. Ever.

We cultivated a rich social life with other actors on *Love of Life* and were having a great time attending their poker parties. The games were half serious, with laughter and teasing fun being the main goal. These gatherings were reminiscent of the good times we had playing cards with the Savalases. That is until an actor, who was doing a brief stint on the show, got wind of our games and asked if he could play. He always arrived with an expensive dessert, lost heavily most of the evening, but at the last hour won all of our money. Someone noticed this pattern and wondered if he might be a professional and it seemed he just might. But since we all worked together, it was impossible to exclude him. So we laughed at our naivete and began to "fold" during the last hour. If someone stayed "in" with three aces and lost, they took weeks of unmerciful teasing.

It was a privilege to be embraced by this "family" of talented people who bent over backwards to make us feel at home. When the director learned that I was also an actress, they gave me a small part as a nurse and regularly called me to work the show. The schedule for taping was during the same hours as school, which allowed me to be home when the kids were. Remarkable! In addition to all the other good things, I could actually return to work and still be a full-time mother. Does life get any better?

New York turned out to be less menacing than the warnings, and the children were doing well. Johnny impressed the teachers with his good mind and extraordinary writing talent, but his real love was football. Excitement filled our house when they accepted him on the team. John had gone to watch a game when he kicked the ball eighty yards! "Mom, I'm so glad John was there, otherwise no one will ever believe I kicked a ball that many yards!" It was an impressive play.

Jennifer was making new friends and we rarely came home from her school without one or two classmates. The play often erupted in squabbles over the never-ending need to decide just who was best friends with whom. My role as referee took on new dimensions. I longed for the backyards of California where children could be consigned to work out their own issues in the democracy of play.

There was Lyle, a boy we often brought home to play. When Johnny was a child, unlike the girls, "best friend" had never been an issue and the play was infinitely more peaceful. I found it to be the same with this boy. Lyle's mother, Dana, divorced and raising her son alone, was going to school to get a degree in art history. She was grateful for the free time to study.

One day I passed the open door to Jennifer's room and overheard the play. Apparently it was a modern version of the old game of "house." I heard Lyle say, "It's time to get a divorce." In a bewildered tone Jennifer said, "Okay." The pretend father then offered a plan: she could have the kids for six months each year and he for the other six. There was a long, silent pause before Jen replied, "Why don't we just make up and keep the family together?" I recalled how often I'd thought that myself. It was sad to learn that playing house had changed to playing divorce.

When Dana came to get her son, I mentioned that our kids played "divorce" today. She was an intelligent woman with a great sense of humor and began to linger more often as we exchanged stories about our lives. I told her about Mother's recent death and a brief history of my childhood. She showed sincere interest and a gentle, yet direct kindness. We were becoming friends.

During one of our visits, Dana confided that her field of study wasn't what she really wanted and expressed a hidden desire to become a doctor. Hadn't she told the right person! I launched into the whole saga of John and medical school, Greece and all. As the tale unfolded, her enthusiasm grew and her eyes widened even more when I ended with my usual, "You can do it if you want to badly enough."

She insisted that there were too many obstacles and listed them one by one. Not one to be discouraged by obstacles, I suggested ways to overcome them, one by one. She balked at government support and food stamps, but I convinced her that assistance programs were meant for people like her, and that a doctor would give back many times more to society. She shouldn't let false pride stand in the way. With a couple of grants she could make it. I offered to baby-sit Lyle.

Dana was easier to convince than John had been, but I was just as proud when she switched to premed at Columbia University, and even more so when she was accepted to medical school. We often had Lyle and Dana join us for dinner. When medical school meant moving out of state, Jennifer felt as though she were losing a sibling.

Studying medicine is grueling work, so it wasn't surprising that we lost touch. A few years later, I was walking with a friend in Greenwich Village and ran into Dana as she was on lunch break from the resident's program at a nearby hospital. There she stood in hospital whites, with a stethoscope around her neck and a name-tag saying "doctor." I blushed when she told my friend that I get full credit for her becoming a doctor. It spoke well of her character that she so generously overstated the small part I played.

One of the benefits of living in New York was that the Greek side of the family lived only a short two-hour turnpike ride away and we could make frequent visits. It was wonderful to watch the kids become so connected with Greek culture and to participate in its customs. Johnny had a natural ability with language and tried to increase the Greek he'd recently learned. I enjoyed being part of a family, sharing a meal with John's, and knowing that I, too, belonged. It made me happy when they called Jennifer "our" baby. I never grew tired of Yaya's stories about Crete and her most cherished memories of watching the sea from her bedroom window in the morning. I had seen that window and that sea.

John became more sweetly affectionate. We walked the streets of New York or waited for our elevator with his arm lovingly holding mine. He never failed to enter or leave a room without displaying his feelings with a hug or a kiss. People often referred to us as the newlyweds. More than anything I loved the way his eyes smiled when he spoke to me. He was working at what he loved. Happiness overflowed in me.

As Johnny moved deeper into his teens, he gradually outgrew the desire to socialize with us. He preferred to stay at home. We knew that he was beginning to separate from us. Jennifer still wanted a lot of attention, but Johnny was my firstborn and it was hard to watch him slip away into adulthood.

I decided to make a standing date with my son for a monthly dinner in the neighborhood restaurant. It gave us a chance to be alone and to talk without little sister interrupting. Our meals together turned out to be good preparation for his dating years. He would pull out my chair as I sat, order our food, and pay the check with money I slipped into his hand. We had interesting talks and I thought he was one of the best dates I ever had. When dinner was over and it was time to leave, he politely held my coat while other diners smiled as we left. I cherished the experience of watching my son become a man.

A year and a half later our special dates ended. Johnny's grades were so good that the school graduated him in mid-winter. I knew that he hadn't adjusted to life in New York City and really hated the cold weather, but I wasn't prepared for what happened next.

The words hit like bullets. The kitchen counter caught my weight as a nervous seventeen-year-old boy spelled out his plan. He began with the assurance that this wasn't personal. He hated New York, he missed California, and his dad really needed him in Texas. He planned to spend a few months helping his father

126

adjust to a second and recent divorce and then continue west to attend college in California. He reminded me that I had often told him that people can do anything if they want to badly enough, and this was what he wanted. It's funny how kids can take your own words and turn them back on you. He added that he loved me and the family very much, but he desperately missed the warm sunshine in Los Angeles.

I didn't try to change his mind. I held him and mentioned my surprise that he'd be leaving home, but that we'd help when it was possible if this was what he wanted. It must have taken a lot of courage for such a young man to hit the road and I worried about his safety. Then I remembered that I, too, had left home at seventeen.

The years with my son had been too few and, like countless other parents, I was heartbroken until I remembered something about children that I once read in a book by Kahlil Gibran. These words of wisdom had become my resolve many years earlier when a friend gave me *The Prophet* as a gift.

> Your children are not your children. They are the sons and daughters of Life's longing for itself. They come through you but not from you. And though they are with you yet they belong not to you. For their souls dwell in the house of tomorrow which you cannot visit, not even in your dreams.

I knew it was time for Johnny to head out for that house of tomorrow where, until now, only his soul dwelt.

For the first time in her nine years of life, Jenny felt the sadness of losing someone she loved. She insisted that I try to talk him out of it. I told her he needed to become a man and must go. She said that Daddy was a man and he could be one here, too.

All too soon Johnny was in Texas and we had to content ourselves with weekly phone calls. He was discovering girls, making new friends, working various jobs, and getting to know bachelor life with his father.

When it was time for the move to Los Angeles, he bought an old car and drove there with three other friends. It was a trip from hell, fraught with car trouble, unexpected floods, and terrible weather. Disheveled and exhausted, he finally arrived on the doorstep of his favorite aunt and uncle in Los Angeles. He was growing up fast and in a few months he found a part-time job and rented an apartment. In the meantime, we tried to fill the void in our lives.

Jennifer didn't say much, but I knew by the sadness in her eyes that she missed her brother. When the musical *Annie* came to town, I thought a Broadway show might lift her spirits. She was very excited when I told her that we had tickets, but I don't think she really understood what was actually meant by a stage production with live actors. When the curtain went up, Jennifer was spellbound. From the first word spoken, her attention was riveted onto the actors until the final curtain fell. I couldn't recall a time when I had seen her so totally captivated.

During intermission, my nine-year-old's excitement burst forth: "On television people are small, get turned on and off, and don't seem real. Are they Mommy? Oh yeah, Daddy's real," she said. In school, acting was part of play, but here were grown-ups doing it on a stage. Wow! There were real people singing, dancing, and acting out a story like they do with fairy tales in school!

As we left the theater, Jenny held my arm and confided with mature determination that she was going to do that when she grew up. In the years to come, I never once saw her waver from that goal. The voice of destiny had spoken and Jenny heard every word.

For days *Annie* was the topic of conversation in school and there was new enthusiasm for story-time acting. Jenny loved school and I was grateful that the Waldorf method impressed John enough to include the tuition in our budget.

At some point I was asked to chaperon class outings and my volunteer spirit complied. Sharing adventures added to Jen's excitement. There were trips to the South Street Seaport; various museums, such as the Metropolitan or The Cloisters; school fairs and other activities; along with a constant stream of class outings, birthday parties, play dates, lessons, and the like, that were often exhausting. But I was happy to be involved. I got to be included in what other parents only hear about at dinner.

One day I answered the telephone and heard a familiar voice say "Deal the cards." It was Telly and I knew that greeting meant let's play bridge. He would be staying in Manhattan to tape background scenes for *Kojak* and wanted to make a date immediately. He teasingly warned that his game had improved after some coaching from two expert players, Omar Shariff and Burt Lancaster, and we needed to read our Goren on Bridge guide to keep him from getting bored.

John and I hadn't played since Greece and were feeling eager as we entered the lobby of his sublet apartment on the east side. A beautiful blonde woman that we hadn't yet met greeted us warmly at the door and the bridge was great. It soon became evident that Telly's game had improved considerably, but the evening was different. Something was definitely missing. Of course, it was Lynn.

A year or so before we left California, the Savalases' marriage had ended. That divorce was a blow to all of us who loved them like family. I was further upset when Lynn's lovely face bore traces of a broken heart. I imagined her sitting in the library at her desk by the window, wondering how she could live with the pain. I thought of her gazing at the gardens across the street, absorbing the shock and trying to decide what to do to help her two sad little girls. Now here I was, playing cards in the wake of their breakup and it just didn't feel right. We loved Telly, we loved bridge, but we went home early and didn't play cards again.

When Lynn's eldest daughter, Penelope, moved to Manhattan years later, we all shared Thanksgiving. Lynn and Telly happily ate Penelope's delicious turkey together. A solid friendship had grown out of a basic respect for each other's role in their children's lives, which made life easier for everyone.

I was beginning to love the city, with its frantic pace, and found that my own speed had increased. When I finally overcame my fear of yellow cabs, driving became a wonderful adventure. Taxi drivers used to honk first but now I did and I drove even faster when they gave me the finger. I enjoyed window shopping in the beautiful stores of Manhattan, planning for the day when it was time to buy things like china and crystal. John said we needed to wait for expensive things, but it was fun to look anyway.

John was gaining popularity on *Love of Life*, but we bemoaned the fact that his story-line didn't include a love interest, and we had been hoping for some time that the writers might create one. Love engenders audience appeal for the character, and when John came home with the news that they were auditioning women for just that purpose, we were ecstatic. I hoped that she'd be very beautiful but nervously hoped that she wouldn't.

I kept my friend Molly informed of our news, the most recent being the talk between John and Nick, a crew member

130

friend, of opening a restaurant. I didn't tell her that John was being hesitant because, when it came to trying something new, he usually was. But between his friend and I, we talked him into opening a restaurant we called the Fives. They found a space right across the street from the studio and negotiated a wonderful lease. When summer came, John's romantic story-line was moving right along and the Fives was nearly ready to open.

I saw very little of my husband because he was either working on the show or supervising the construction of the restaurant as raw space was being turned into an elegant dining area. It seemed a perfect idea when John suggested that since school was out soon, Jennifer and I should have a nice visit in California.

By now Johnny had filled his apartment with most of the items we had stored. It was quite an experience to see my son in his home with things that had previously been in mine. Friends had helped decorate and the place looked quite nice. Jennifer found that at nine years old she now had more in common with her big brother and he adored taking her places. They grew closer as Jen managed to share her brother's obsession with the Dallas Cowboys, spurred on by the fact that their training camp was in the west valley. One day he took her to a training session and Johnny convinced those big guys to come over to meet his little sister and to take pictures with her. It was a thrilling day and I heard more about it, in greater detail, when the photos came back from the store.

It was wonderful to return to California where everyone was happy for John's success and that everything had turned out so well for us. By now we were seasoned New Yorkers and had many stories to tell. There was great interest in hearing what life was like in that "scary" city, but few of my L.A. friends could imagine living there.

As had been our custom for years, my sisters and I gathered around the kitchen table to reminisce about the childhood we all had survived. There was always humor in the retelling. When we remembered how our dignified father lost his teeth on the lawn, we laughed until our sides hurt. Jen hung onto every word and adored these times with her aunts.

There was only time for two visits with Lynn, but I could see that she had rebuilt her life and that Candace and Penelope were well-adjusted, splendid young women.

Our good news brought tears to Molly's eyes, but she was worried because I had booked our return to New York on the same day as the restaurant opening. When she came to watch me pack and to spend a few final minutes together, I reassured her that a car was meeting us at the airport and there was nothing to worry about. As I filled the suitcase, she sat on the bed and told me how deeply grateful she was to see me so happy. She wanted me to know that if she'd ever seemed impatient in those difficult years, it was only because she loved me so much. Johnny came home from work to take us to the airport and when he went to put our things in the car, Molly and I hugged each other and we knew that ours were tears of joy.

When Jen and I arrived at Kennedy airport in New York, there was just half an hour to make the opening. The car was on time but it took two hours to find our lost luggage and the evening was about to be spoiled. The driver phoned John about our problem and they delayed the opening as long as they could, but he was finally forced to start without us. By the time we arrived, dinner was over and I hadn't even had time to change. John's leading lady was there in a brown silk dress and gave a rose to Jenny and me. She had been sitting with Yaya who was now at our table and had also been given a rose. When John sat next to me, he leaned over with clear admiration and whispered that the brown silk dress had cost eight hundred dollars. I glanced down at my polyester print travel skirt and wanted to crawl under the table. I spent the rest of the evening knowing he'd never let me spend that much on a dress and wondering why he was impressed by the extravagance.

The next morning John left for work early. I went down a few minutes later to catch a bus to do errands and saw him climbing into a cab. I had only enough change for the bus and wondered if he always took cabs. I thought of the many times I'd been forced to return home because I was hungry and didn't even have enough money for coffee.

Later that night I told him I needed my own checking account. When he asked why, I told him I was always out of cash. He jokingly pulled out his money clip and handed me dollar bills one at a time. I forced myself to laugh at his joke then said, "No, I need to have my own money." He wouldn't budge from his adamant no and I was firm in my intention to never force him to do anything again. Ever.

But I was left without money of my own and John was in control of ours.

Chapter 10
"I'M NOT COMMITTED TO THIS MARRIAGE"

ESIGNERS WERE ALREADY DRESSING STORE windows for the unsurpassed beauty of Christmas in New York. It was midautumn of the third year since the move east, and the air was crisp and getting colder. The city had unveiled many of its mysteries and I was no longer afraid to take part in its magic. I loved walking to do errands, smiling at strangers, and was pleasantly surprised when they smiled back. I delighted in the friendly neighborhood atmosphere one doesn't experience in the automobile life of southern California. The changing seasons were glorious and there was always something new to discover. I felt alive with anticipation.

Each day passed in sharp contrast to the life we left behind in California. After we married, John came to live in my home bringing a few tattered clothes, an old car, and a dream of becoming a star. Our move east had forced me to store most of my things in Los Angeles in order to follow his dream, which by now had become ours. That dream was coming true in this magical city, and the past was left way behind.

People on the street began to recognize John, which is always a good sign for an actor. We were becoming a popular couple with fan magazine buyers, which attracted journalists to our home for interviews and photo sessions. We felt happy when relatives saw pictures of our family or read stories about us in magazines. An article appeared in a fan magazine that pleased me to no end. The writer gave a detailed account of an extraordinary actor who had gone to medical school. It described John as so vital and energetic that he had refused to sit around waiting for acting jobs, so he decided to remodel a house. Then, when that was finished, he went to medical school. I observed to myself that John really would have preferred to sit around and wait for acting jobs, but was pleased to find a positive interpretation of the activities I had forced upon him. It didn't matter that I was given no credit because pushing John to do things against his will hadn't left me feeling very attractive and I hoped that the article meant I looked good in my husband's eyes. It was true that John had accomplished the implementation and that's the important thing. A smile hit my mood.

Nothing could diminish that smile, not even the high cost of living that kept me juggling finances or the fact that there was still a lot lacking in our house. The romantic story-line for John's television character had increased his popularity and we were expecting a raise in salary soon. *Love of Life* had suddenly stopped calling me to play a nurse and I wanted to find a way to bring in some money. We had expected the restaurant to add to our income, but John said it was slow getting the Fives off the ground. I offered to work there part time. In addition to earning a salary, I could give that personal touch to customer relations. John said no. I insisted. He insisted harder. He continued to make all the decisions.

A longing to discover the meaning of life and to know why things happen had led me to discover concepts such as reincarnation and karma. I'd come to believe that before we're born we choose our destiny. I wondered about mine.

Since Mother's death, I had been pondering the fact that my youngest sister and I had many similar qualities, but also many that were quite different. How would I have turned out if I'd been the one Mother kept behind? Without the regular dose of Father's rage, would my own problems with anger be less? Would I have had the tenacity to stick it out in California? If it's true that experiences are connected, mine seemed to culminate in this wonderful new existence.

Johnny was happy in California with school, a job, and catching rays in the sun. In his phone calls there were vague references to a new girlfriend. Big John was living his dream and was sorry that the restaurant took so much of his time. Jennifer was bursting with excitement about the birthday party of Mary Sayles, her "best friend," which had been the preoccupation of the children for weeks. It was clearly the social event of the fourth-grade class. The day before the party I bought the present and hurried to pick Jennifer up from school. "Mommy, the party's tomorrow morning!" Her delightfully expectant mood filled the car and swept me along, too. It was as if the little girl in me had awakened for a brief moment to experience my child's joy. As we wrapped the gift, I felt gratitude for the many times I'd been privileged to experience the wonder of childhood through my daughter.

Jennifer said she was too excited to eat as I started dinner. I waited for the phone call that came every evening at five. A warm, tender voice would say "Hello, Mrs. Aniston, this is your husband, I'm on my way home, do you need anything from the store?" He'd arrive home around six, like clockwork each day, with or without missing supplies. I was hopelessly smug and secure in the love of my wonderful, dependable husband—until the day before the birthday party when his five o'clock call didn't come.

At seven o'clock, with still no word, I tried to coax Jennifer to eat as I wondered if John was okay. I made another phone call to the restaurant and was reassured that he'd be home soon. Jenny didn't eat much for dinner and when I put her to bed, we sat for a long time talking about the big event in the morning. Would she win a prize? She really didn't care; the party would be wonderful enough. Each time I tried to leave the room there was just one more thing to say and sleep was a long time coming that night.

Nine o'clock and still no word from John. Worried, I sat down to distract myself in a television movie. The story was about a man who had been paralyzed in an accident and asked his wife for a divorce so he wouldn't be a burden to her. She loved him, the children needed their father, and she tearfully refused. My attention was held as I watched this story, in a way so reminiscent of my own situation. As the wife refused to divorce I identified with her reasoning that love was enough to keep them together. Around ten o'clock John came home. I suggested that he come and watch the program because it reminded me of us. He said he'd been thinking and sat down. I asked if it couldn't wait until the end of the movie. He sat next to me on the couch. We watched as the story ended with a promise from the husband to never mention divorce again, and both committed to their love. Tears were streaming down my face as I turned to John and said that the woman reminded me of my own fierce determination to keep our family together while we struggled to overcome the blocks in his way. I was taken aback when he said, "I don't remember it that way."

I asked, "You don't remember what that way?" When no answer came, I shrugged it off and told him about an idea I'd had for a while: "You know, I've been thinking, why don't we get remarried and have a big wedding this time?"

"No, that's not a good idea."

I said, "Please, don't you think it would be nice? I really want to."

The conversation that followed was oddly surrealistic and hard to understand. John was vague and talked about things that made no sense to me. I asked questions for clarity but it wasn't helping. Finally he mumbled that he wasn't committed to the marriage. I asked him what exactly that meant and he repeated it again. He asked if I remembered that he didn't want to get married and I said it was he who talked me into it. Then I tried to figure out how that issue related to our conversation. John was still sounding strange and unclear so I got up and walked to the window, where nearly two years ago I had absorbed the news of Mother's death, and was surprised to see the first faint light of morning. We'd been talking all night and I still didn't know what he was trying to say. A question popped into my head, so I turned to him and heard myself forming the unthinkable words, "Are you trying to ask for a divorce?" It shocked me to the core when he answered yes.

No. NO! It screamed loud in my head but no sound came out of my mouth. I turned back to the window in silence and noticed early risers snapping on lights to start their day. I wanted to fly out the window, high over the city, to escape the reality of that yes, but instead I asked, "Why?"

"I'm not committed to the marriage" was all the response John gave.

"Is that all you're going to say?" I needed to hear more.

"I don't like yelling."

"What?" It flew out, then more calmly I said, "I don't like it either but until you went back to school it was the only way to get you out of bed. For the past few years you've been doing your part and there's been no yelling."

He said it was too late, he wasn't happy, there was nothing more to say, and that he'd be leaving soon.

I asked when, and he said, "Now, today."

At that moment, strange as it sounds, all I could think about was the birthday party that meant so much to Jen. I told him that at eleven o'clock this morning there was going to be a birthday party that Jennifer had been looking forward to for weeks and this news will spoil it for her. I asked if he would wait until tomorrow. John agreed to wait until she was at the party but was determined to leave that day. I was quite aware that it's easier to get a rhinoceros to dance on my toilet than to get John to change his mind, so I stopped trying and he went to get some sleep in Johnny's old room. A terrible sensation settled in my stomach. A massive lump constricted my throat, and every muscle in my body went into spasm.

Soon Jennifer would be getting up and her heart would be breaking like mine. It would take all of my will to match her festive mood. Somehow I managed to maintain my composure through breakfast and on the drive to the east-side apartment of her friend. The children were adorable in their party clothes and squealed with delight to see Jennifer as Mary Sayles's mother invited us in. Jen ran off with a group blowing party favors at each other.

Cassie Sayles said I looked pale and when I began to cry, she ushered me into a sitting room. I apologized and felt the need to tell her briefly what had just happened. Cassie said, "Don't worry, I've been there, too." She insisted I sit a while to get myself together and came in from time to time to offer words of comfort. I listened with interest as she told, bit by bit, of a terrible divorce from a soap actor husband who had left her for his leading lady. That's not the case here, I assured with confidence, and realized I had to go. I kissed my daughter good-bye and was glad that her turn in a game caused a distraction that hid my tears.

I ran to the car and collapsed in a heap until the crying subsided. When I got home, John was standing in the living room wearing his fine new clothes with packed suitcases near the door. A voice that was mine asked if he was sure he wanted to do this. He said yes. I reminded him of all I'd been through for so many years and he answered, "I think you're trying to make me feel guilty." I resisted the desire to say, well yes, and instead said, "It isn't fair." He answered that nobody said life was fair. I whispered that this couldn't be happening and felt myself falling apart. When I heard him say, with eerie resignation, "Your dreams didn't come true, Nancy," I knew he'd better go. With forced courage I mentioned that the goal I'd had since we first joined together was that he have what he wanted, so if he really wanted to go, I'd find a way to want it, too. He picked up his suitcases, wished me the best and for the first time since we met, left without kissing me good-bye.

As the door was closing, I gave one more try and called out, "Can't we just separate and get some counseling? I love you, and Jennifer needs to grow up in a family." As he walked away, John said no, that he was going for good and would not be coming back. The door closed. It's not clear how long I stood on that spot feeling the ground disappear. Then, for some strange reason I went to his closet to see if it was empty. Perhaps if something was left he'd have to come home. But there were only empty hangers dangling there. He entered my life with practically nothing and left it with everything he wanted most, including the dream that was ours.

I let myself sink into a space deep inside and for hours I just sat thinking of the innocent little girl playing a party game, not knowing the news that waited at home. It was sheer agony. I shed torrents of tears. Telling a child that a parent is leaving must be one of the most difficult tasks a human being can be asked to perform and I frantically searched for a concept that would make it easier for her. It was up to me to help her handle news that even I could hardly bear, news that in a perfect world no child should have to hear. When it came right down to it, I knew it would be impossible to tell her the whole truth, so I decided to tell a white lie. I would tell her that Daddy had some problems so he moved out for a while to think things over. When she could handle the moving out, the never coming back might be easier to take. It was one of the very few times I have lied to either of my children.

At four in the afternoon it was time to pick up Jen. I hid my swollen face behind dark glasses and stopped at the market to buy a pack of cigarettes. It was the second time I started that terrible habit and it continued another five years.

As soon as we got home I chose the edited version to tell. I watched a tear roll down Jenny's cheek as confidence faded from her once trusting eyes. Confusion and faint lines of worry broke prematurely into her innocent face as the news sank in. When she started to cry I held her tight, and I knew from the shaking that the lie was all she could take. I rocked my sad bundle, stroked her hair, and repeated "It's all right. Everything's going to be all right" as the two of us sat there crying. We talked about what our life would be like, and I silently hoped that I had never been, or ever would be, the cause of such agony.

The next two weeks passed in a dark cloud of shock as the joy, so long in coming, slipped away. My single most important mission was to prevent a complete breakdown. I had to be there for Jen. With my every muscle in total spasm, food wouldn't go down and sleep was impossible. A kind of rhythm developed as if I were performing a part in a play. I was the cheerful mother with Jen, but when she was absent, I reverted to the grieving, dumped wife.

One thing was clear: I had lost forever any chance to achieve that childhood dream of having a traditional family one day and I knew that it was lost for Jen as well. When I was the same age as she, the death of my favorite little sister had shaken the foundation of trust in life for me. It was imperative that I find a way to rebuild my nine-year-old daughter's trust.

Each morning the mom she was used to packed lunch in a brown paper bag (cooler than those childish metal pails with pictures of Barbie on them). It became a ritual on the drive to school to reach for the bag to see what picture I'd drawn on it that day. Was it a Santa, a Christmas tree, or a cuddly brown bear? I used my talent for drawing as part of my effort to fill her days with surprises so that she might not notice the void. The next phase of the morning began after our usual kiss good-bye and she disappeared into school. My tears started flowing and didn't stop until it was time to pick her up. I regained composure and maintained it through dinner and bedtime, but as soon as the door to her room closed, the flood gates opened and my sobs continued until morning. Time with Jennifer was normal, but time alone didn't exist. I wondered how anyone could hurt that much or cry that many tears.

Johnny was peacefully living in California. When I told him that John wanted a divorce, it surprised me that my grown son cried, too, and asked me what he should do. I suggested he go on loving John as much as ever and that when everything settled they'd be connected again.

But I couldn't rebound from the shock. Doing ordinary chores was often impossible. When I went to the market I found myself selecting items that were favorites of John and Little Johnny. I put it all back and left without groceries. I wasn't eating and Jen had take-out that night.

By the time Thanksgiving arrived, I was able to swallow food and persuaded John to join us for dinner in a neighborhood restaurant. This was the first time we'd been together since the separation, and it felt odd when he withheld the hello kiss I was used to or didn't slip his arm around me in the usual way, and the warm look in his eyes had turned so cold it made me shiver. I wondered why he was mad at me. Throughout dinner Little Jenny tried to be especially charming so that Daddy might want to come home. But he was awkward and fidgety and I was pretty sure he wouldn't join us for another holiday. I knew I'd have to expand myself to be all of the family Jennifer needed.

When we got home, John made a hasty retreat and I knew we wouldn't see him at Christmas. The tone for the future was set.

Our favorite holiday would soon be here and I needed to find a way to make it special. The traditions we'd known were gone and it was important to create new ones. There would only be two of us exchanging gifts so I decided to prepare a spectacular display by putting aside every new purchase to wrap, no matter how silly. Even if it were a dish towel or a new can opener, it still got wrapped to make sure that both of us would be opening packages Christmas morning.

The plan was taking shape. I'd heard that dinner at Tavern on the Green in Central Park is sheer magic on Christmas Eve. The dining rooms are exquisitely decorated with garlands, reindeer, poinsettias, and little white lights shine everywhere. I made reservations early and told Jenny we were going to do something very special. When it was time to get dressed, we put on our lovely new clothes and told each other we looked quite stunning. As we entered the room her little face glowed at the sight and Jen said, "Wow, this is the most beautiful place I've ever seen." A man wearing tails showed us to our table with a clear view of the big Christmas tree at the far end of the room, where carolers sang and French doors framed trees with bare branches covered with snow. Waiters in tuxedos doted on our every wish and we felt like two little queens. Adding the perfect touch to a magical evening, Robert Reed, the actor who played the father on Jennifer's favorite show, *The Brady Bunch*, sat at the table next to ours. She stole glances all night but couldn't summon the courage to approach him directly and tried to convince me to do it.

After dinner Jennifer requested an ice cream cone for dessert, so we drove to the shop near our home. It was raining and cold so I kept the car running while she ran inside to get the treats. A woman wearing shiny lipstick stood under a large, black umbrella and knocked on the car, so I lowered the window to see what she wanted. It was impossible to hear a word in that rain and I was trying to interpret her gestures when my daughter appeared with an ice cream cone in each little hand. The woman took a step back, looked at Jen, at me, at the cones, at me again, and broke into a large crimson grin as she backed away under that umbrella, repeating, "I'm sorry, so sorry, real sorry."

On the drive home I realized that I had parked at what was rumored to be a well-serviced hooker spot. Apparently the woman was working that night and maybe she thought I wanted company on Christmas Eve. It made me sad to think how she would spend the holiest night of the year.

When we had eaten our ice cream and Jennifer was sound asleep, I quietly placed a mountain of beautifully wrapped gifts under our tree. The next morning began early with the usual dash to the presents and Jen's reaction was even better than I'd expected. But it was time for something new to begin, so we put off unwrapping just yet. We were creating a celebration that belonged to the two of us. I lit a candle and suggested we take a moment to sit quietly with our hot chocolate and talk about the real meaning of gift giving. Jennifer's eyes glowed with wonder as she listened to a description of the grandness of a Spirit that sacrifices for others out of love, and that the gifts we receive are just a small reminder that the greatest gift of all is to give of ourselves. We thanked God for the abundance of good in our lives and laughed at some of the silly presents. Jennifer said it was the best Christmas she'd ever had.

We had started a yearly tradition of dinner in the Crystal Room at Tavern on the Green but were never there alone again. It became part of the treat to see what special friends would join us. When Jenny's godsister, Penelope, lived in New York, she was with us for some of our happiest times. One year Jennifer said that no matter how old she was or where she was living, she would always want to celebrate Christmas with me in just that way. It was pure grace that in the middle of devastating loss we found a beauty and magic in Christmas that lasted for many years. I'm sure it was just one of the miracles that special season.

The new year began with a wonderful blanket of snow to cover the city, which hid the more undesirable aspects of proximity. The sky was a glorious blue with fluffy white clouds and resembled a renaissance painting. We were rising out of the rubble by taking it a day at a time.

Jennifer began asking when Daddy would come home and I felt it was time to tell her he wouldn't. Taking the last vestige of hope away would be a final blow from this unwanted divorce. When I told her that he would never come home, she cried and said, "Mommy, I can't believe I'm going to be one of those kids who grows up without a father." Recalling the game of "divorce" she had played with her friend not long before, I wondered if she had intuited the possibility even then.

We hadn't seen much of John that year and never once reached him at the place he was staying. When he finally did call, it was painful to watch Jenny chatter on, trying to entice him to stay on the phone. He was a busy man who had to rush off and the hang-up always came far too soon. She'd flash a brave smile and run off to hide the tears in her room. I never knew when to follow or when to leave her alone.

For me, sleepless nights continued and the long hours were endless, so I'd do cleaning chores to pass the night. About three o'clock one morning I was defrosting the freezer when I heard the front door open and a few beats later John walked into the kitchen. He looked quite dashing in his new cashmere coat as he stood gazing at me in my rubber gloves and the old granny nightgown he hated. It was clear who had come a long way and equally clear who hadn't.

He went to get some papers from our bedroom and when he came out, I said, "This is too hard to do without knowing why or what happened, so can't we please have a few sessions with a therapist?" It was an unexpected surprise when he agreed to one session only, so I refrained from asking for his key.

A friend recommended a woman who specialized in couple counseling. When I made the appointment, she suggested I come early to fill in some history before John arrived. There was just enough time to tell her that I had no idea what caused the breakup because all he would say was that he wasn't committed to the marriage.

"What else?" she wondered.

"That's all. He keeps insisting there's no one else." Then the buzzer signaled his arrival.

The doctor restated my question, saying, "Nancy told me you've left the marriage and she really needs to know why."

In his same quiet tone, John said that he wasn't committed to the marriage.

When she asked if that was all he had to say, John replied, "There's really nothing more to say."

She tried several approaches with no luck and then suggested he might as well go. I stayed to talk for a while, hoping for some encouragement, but it was useless. When a trained therapist wasn't able to drag any more out of him than I could, it was clear he really had no more to say. I never saw that therapist again.

Our friend Daren Kline wrote a play and invited me to a reading. A lot of people were there. John read one of the parts and it felt odd to be there with him, yet without him. Soon it was over, and afterward I told Daren that the play was interesting; as a gesture of friendship he asked how I was doing. When my eyes filled with tears, Daren invited himself over to dinner. He arrived that night with a bottle of wine, made a big fuss over my spaghetti, and said I was still the most beautiful woman he knew. Since Daren was openly gay and not making a pass, I took it as a compliment and allowed my damaged ego to rebound. He added that one of the actors at the reading thought I was beautiful, too, and wondered if I was interested in having a date. It was flattering but I had to decline. Then I confided that this sudden and unexpected loss was excruciatingly painful and that I wanted to take some time to understand why.

"But he wants to 'do' you, and wouldn't that be a great distraction?"

"That's the point," I said, "I don't want to be distracted until I know what destiny is trying to say."

The look on his face betrayed that he thought I was crazy. He then said that for so long he had been dying to 'do' that same guy. We moved to the couch to sip brandy, smoke, and to quietly continue our chat.

At one point he asked, "Darling, what is going on with John and that girl from the show?"

"Nothing," I laughed, "Why?"

He said that they had been seen all over town together.

No, not the girl in the brown silk dress who gave me, Jenny, and Yaya roses?

Daren recalled that he'd asked that same question a few months ago and I had exactly the same reaction.

I started to tear and said, "So who's the biggest denial dodo you know?"

"So now will you 'do' that actor?"

"No."

It felt as though I had just been robbed. You start picturing a stranger in your house, using your bathroom, your bed, and your husband. She's tasting your porridge, and eating it all up and you begin to cry. Goldilocks had been sleeping in my bed and I was the last to know. I thought of Cassie Sayles's question at the children's party that day. Had she intuited something or are these the unbeatable odds? Once the blinders came off, there were tales of sightings everywhere and a lot of pieces began to fit in. I understood why Nurse Nancy didn't get called by the show, why I couldn't work in our restaurant, and especially why we didn't have enough money. You know, as hard as it was, as trashed as I felt, it was still a relief to know why.

John had boiled it down to simply "I'm not committed to the marriage." That well-worn phrase took on new meaning and was, undeniably, just about the whole truth.

Many people said they had witnessed the two as a couple and our employees in the restaurant added that she usually came there with John. When I told him I knew and that he might as well tell me, he flat out denied it. But time didn't support that lie.

Jen still wanted to know if Daddy would come home. I kept reminding her, no. There had been no answer at his telephone number and now I knew why. We dined in our restaurant and Jenny asked a waiter if, when he saw her daddy, he could please ask him to call. My eyes filled with tears as I wondered what to tell her. It's a complicated web we human beings weave. Our family was happy, but John wasn't happy with me, so he got happy with her, and now Jen and I aren't happy at all. A trade off was made that in my book gave "happy" a bad name.

I thought it over carefully and decided that the truth of where John preferred to be would be withheld from Jenny for the time being. I knew that no matter what my feelings were, for the sake of protecting Jenny's future relationships with men, I didn't want her to know that her father was with another woman. I vowed I would always find a way to reflect a good image of him. She had enough burdens to overcome and it was better this way.

All hope of reconciliation was gone. Jen continued to miss Daddy, which was worsened by missing her brother. It became my main concern to make sure that Jennifer knew, beyond all doubt, that I would never leave her and that she could always count on me to be there. Nothing took precedence over that. To be even more reassuring, I took her everywhere with me. Together we trooped through the city, occasionally laughing at absurdities and in follow-up discussions at home. There gradually developed a communality of understanding between us for much that went on. In that close, warm unfolding we began to heal.

Chapter 11
CARVING UP A LIFE

IT WAS MY GOOD FORTUNE that I managed to hide the true extent of my own suffering from Jen. But as soon as I was alone, an avalanche of dark thoughts pounded my brain. Like falling rocks, there was no stopping them. Where were the warnings, the complaints, or the hint of discontent? Where was the period to adjust after so many years? Why was there no indication of John's unhappiness before it was too late? And wasn't I dumber than dirt not to have seen it coming? The rocks continued falling day after day, week after week until I hated the sniveling, self-pitying victim I found myself becoming. I didn't want to go there, but it would have been easier to stop an avalanche than to change the course human nature was charting for me.

My dreams didn't come true. Who said life is fair? I had to dig deep for strength to hang on. At times it felt as if the core of my being

153

was trying to escape through the top of my head. With my heart pounding and my face covered with sweat, I would hold onto a piece of furniture until the sensation passed.

Each morning I'd drop Jennifer off at school and rush home to pray and meditate, trying to understand how and why. I feared that a part of me was slipping away. Two people had played with fire and my life went up in the flames.

As the first year of our separation was about to end, John said it was time to discuss the divorce. When I said I didn't want one, I felt a slight tremor begin. He pressed hard until my body began to shake all over. Noticing my tenuous state, he mercifully left. I sat a long time staring at nothing. No thinking. No brain. There wasn't much left to even think about starting over.

I was desperate to be near someone who cared, but my sisters and closest friends were all in California. The telephone helped, but I longed for an understanding presence. Some old friends of John's, John and Susan Dooley, lived in our building. We had only socialized as couples and hadn't really spoken intimately. I had noticed a gentle kindness in Susan, but she might feel awkward or forced to take sides. In a moment of desperation I decided none of that mattered. I had to reach out. She received my call warmly and was visibly stunned by the news of my disintegrated marriage. "But it's always been obvious that John adores you!" she said. I bathed my wounded spirit in her sympathetic words as she recalled my years of financial struggle with John. She insisted that some kind of illness had him confused and that it would pass.

A few days later, it was quite moving to hear that she and her husband drove to our restaurant and after circling the block a few times, went in to see if they could find out what was troubling John. They thought the sight of old friends might help. She then expressed regret that John still had nothing to say. They returned home disappointed. I hugged Susan and thanked her. These two people had gone out on a limb for me. Not a dent had been made in my husband's determination, but I would never forget that John and Susan Dooley, with nothing to gain, had made an unselfish human gesture. That took guts.

Susan's big heart was breaking for Jenny, too, and she suggested a practical antidote. We agreed that every little girl needs a beautiful bedroom in which to create her dreams. Susan covered her long blond hair with a Gucci scarf and did most of the work as we turned Jennifer's room into a haven of cheerful yellow and white lace. In just a few weeks it was fit for a princess. Jenny adored the tiny yellow flowers on the wallpaper and her reaction suggested that we both had the same appreciation for beautiful surroundings.

When the room was finished, daily contact with Susan was gone, and those terrible feelings of rejection surfaced again. I'd walk the crowded streets of Manhattan, resisting the temptation to grab a complete stranger's arm to ask, "Have you ever felt this rotten?" It was the self-centered Eighties, more women than ever were getting dumped, and I wondered if others would be willing to share their coping skills. I had read that a whole variety of support groups were springing up and I started looking. On one of my walks I noticed a charming little book store that only sold books about women.

The sun was shining brightly when I walked through the door, and though my eyes couldn't see for a moment, my hopes were high. When the books came into clear focus I glanced around in amazement. To my great surprise the covers displayed all kinds of sexual secrets, positions, and intimate stories of the Lesbian lifestyle. I stepped back and whispered, "Oh." Not one to give up easily and with forced nonchalance, I took a tour of the room. I was determined to find a warm, friendly woman who had lost her man and her family like me. But every last one in the store that day was cold, unfriendly, and not very feminine. I had to admit defeat. On the way home I knew it was time to seek professional help.

I recalled that a new friend, Barbara Callen, practiced emotional therapy. I had admired her wisdom on several occasions, and decided to call for an appointment. I dialed the number wondering if I would always lose everyone I love.

At the same time, the mom in me was happy to notice that Jen's keen interest and enthusiasm for life had not been dampened by pain. Strong social impulses were developing. She was only in fifth grade, yet she made friends easily and with nearly everyone in the Steiner school. The grades ranged from kindergarten to twelfth and she had friends in each one. A genuine love for everyone seemed to pour out of Jennifer's calm, easy, manner. I never knew anyone who had so many friends and there was usually one or more in our home. School was a happy place and an important factor in getting through a difficult time.

Each night at dinner we'd chat about all sorts of things. The empty chairs became less conspicuous. A stream of fascinating thoughts poured from Jenny's observant mind. I was intrigued by her interest in everything and everyone she encountered. Her imagination was boundless and a propensity to use multisyllabic words continued to keep me surprised and quite often amused.

One time during dinner we discovered that talking and eating don't mix. We were discussing the biology lesson that had recently been introduced at school. We marveled at the wonders of the human body. At one point Jennifer choked on a bite of food and broke into a fit of coughing. I rushed to her side and told her to look up while I tried to pat the particle loose. When the convulsions subsided, she grabbed her chest and breathlessly said, "Oh my gosh, something got caught in my Fallopian tube." I held back my laughter and went on to explain why it wasn't likely that food got caught there.

An anatomical description of the Fallopian tubes followed, which led to our first "birds and bees" discussion. She was clearly ready for it as her eyes widened and she hung onto every word, responding with intelligent, well-formed questions for a ten year old. At the end of the discussion, there was a moment of silence to consider the full impact of how babies are made. Then a light went on when the thought hit home and she asked with a child's incredulity, "Did you do that with Daddy?" The more things change the more they stay the same. It was good that she was secure enough to ask something that every child wonders about and in my generation, no one dared ask a parent.

Jennifer was moving back into that place where she felt safe during those early years of life. She turned more and more to me for understanding and I was always searching for comforting words or an outing to distract her attention.

Dr. Inge Dyernfurth was a friend with whom I shared spiritual study. Her international reputation as a brilliant scientist had landed her a job as head of the lab at Columbia Presbyterian Hospital in the Bronx. Her scientific mind and intellectual approach to spiritual matters was admired and appreciated by many, and I was honored when our friendship developed. Inge was an older woman who was never too busy to give words of wisdom to me. One day she invited Jen and me to dinner at her house in the country.

Winter was upon us and the cold air was invigorating on the long drive up the Henry Hudson along the Palisades Parkway. We listened to a tape of show tunes and were excited to hear on the radio that it just might snow. Inge was waiting outside to greet us and was delighted to hear how much we had enjoyed seeing trees with bare branches in silhouette against the gray winter sky. We were treated to a guided tour of the house, viewing its charm with mutual admiration as the rooms filled with the scent of something roasting in the oven.

Our hostess suggested we take a walk before dinner, so we bundled back into our coats. Wanting more of this beauty so lacking in the city, we strolled for over an hour. When Jen ran ahead to gather some sticks, Inge gently asked the question I was expecting. "I know when enough time has passed it won't hurt any more," I responded. Inge agreed that if I continued to think of time as the healer it would help get me through.

We returned chilled to the bone and laughed at each other's red noses. A fantastic meal was served on lace-trimmed white linen, crystal, and silver, near a large bay window. We ate until there was barely room for the delicious desert. To add the perfect touch, a light snow began to fall. A fire was crackling, the snow was falling, warm feelings were everywhere, and no one was talking about pain. Though my friend was old enough to be my mother and I the same years older than Jen, we passed the day enjoying each other and barely noticed the difference in age.

When the sun set and the snowfall began to intensify, we declined Inge's suggestion to spend the night. We walked to the car and upon seeing how much snow had accumulated, we were once again asked to stay the night. For some reason it seemed important for us to go home.

We hadn't been driving long when the snow started coming down so heavily that the wiper blades barely cleared the windows.

Jennifer was getting nervous and held her hands in a fist near her heart, fearing that another car might not see us and crash into ours. She was trying hard not to cry. I tried to convince her not to worry because we were probably the only ones on the road. I just hoped the wiper blades didn't break.

We hadn't yet come to the main highway, and with each turn I seemed to be going deeper into the country. It was impossible to tell road from shoulder and at this point I realized we were lost. Fear almost turned my stomach when I thought of how quickly my little Honda would be covered with snow if we had to spend the night in the car. Seeing a street sign in the high beams, I pulled over. I had to get out of the car to see what it said. Jennifer was terrified and I was pretty scared myself.

I was squinting to read the sign when a man appeared out of nowhere. I nearly jumped out of my skin. "Calm down lady," he said, "I only want to help. Strangers often get lost in this kind of weather and end up at this spot, so I wait here to lead them to the highway." That day we were the lucky strangers and I couldn't have felt more grateful. I scraped off the window, which had by now been covered over, and bounced confidently behind the wheel, saying, "We've been saved!" I pointed to the headlights just flicking on and added that a kind man was showing us the way. A big grin flashed from across the seat and Jen's face glowed in the dark. We followed the car lights and before long the parkway to home was in sight. In a matter of seconds we were on the access road to the main highway home. When we turned to wave our thank yous, there wasn't a car in sight.

Jen had often asked questions like who would fix the toilet if it overflowed. Her concerns made me suspect that she was secretly afraid of our life without Dad. After surviving that bliz-

159

zard, a renewed confidence seemed to settle in and Jen didn't ask those questions again. Perhaps the message had been that even if she felt lost or alone, we would definitely make it home.

John continued to complain about how little money he had and Jennifer and I still lacked many things. I realized that now it would be harder than ever to afford them. I discovered the discount stores in New Jersey that sell designer clothes and household items, often at prices below cost. It became an adventure to rummage through, looking for bargains to get what we needed. Tired and hungry, we'd collapse over lunch.

On one such outing, I saw that Jen's enthusiasm was lagging, and before long I noticed her sitting on the base of a mannequin with her very sad face propped on her knees. At first she didn't want to tell me what was the matter, but when she did I knew it had been hard to put into words. What finally came out was, "I hate that half."

I asked, "What half?"

"That half," she repeated and then burst out with, "That half brother!"

"What half brother?"

I'd forgotten.

"My half brother, that I didn't know was only my half brother and I hate it. Is it really true Mommy? Is Johnny only my half brother?"

Oh boy, who told her that without telling me? Hadn't she always known that Johnny visited a different father in the summer and accepted it without question? I'd honestly thought the "half" thing would never be an issue for us, but apparently someone decided to make it one.

It actually wasn't important who told her because at that moment, in the middle of a children's department, she needed to

160

know exactly what this "half" meant and just which half was her brother. I said all of Johnny was her brother but they had different fathers. I clumsily added that they both had been born in the same mother's body, whose blood was in both of them and had always lived together in the same house. "Love is what counts and 'half' means absolutely nothing in our family," I told her. It was a feeble attempt and I knew it wasn't the denial she so desperately wanted to hear. It was a difficult moment for a child whose life had recently been turned upside down. But we went on with our day and soon found a wonderful skirt that went way out when she spun around. To my surprise she didn't mention a word about having a "half" brother at lunch. She never spoke of it again.

Jenny and I continued to visit Yaya and kept a wonderful connection there. Jen looked up to her teenage cousins and loved to hear the latest news when they started dating boys. She enjoyed watching them apply makeup and hearing that when they were little they had loved to watch me apply mine. I had known those two girls since they were just children and feared the strong possibility that one day the loss of my marriage might take them from me. It was a happy moment when one of them confided that I would always be her "Aunt Nancy."

My mother-in-law had been more like a real mother and I loved to be in her house. The walls and tabletops were adorned with photos of the four of us, as well as some single shots of me. It felt like home and helped maintain some continuity. I was still part of the family. Yaya also showed her love by coming to New York, with a couple of relatives, to tell me to fight for my husband. "Go bring him home," she said. Since her son and I were still married, she couldn't imagine that there would be someone else and I didn't have the heart to tell her.

161

It was hard to get used to a new life while living in the same place where everything had once been so different. For years I'd shared a home with John and there had been a natural division of male chores. It wasn't easy getting used to handling the tasks that had been his, and sometimes they seemed impossible to learn. Auto mechanics had always been a mystery and as with many women, I was pretty uninformed. One day it appeared that I might be forced to overcome my ignorance when it was time to pick up Jen from school and the car had a flat tire. I phoned the restaurant to ask John for help. The manager was sympathetic to my disjointed discourse and said, "Calm down, he's here." After what seemed an eternity, John responded to my call by insisting, in very clear English, that I must learn to handle these things myself. I suggested it might be better if I learned when a child wasn't waiting in front of the school. He arranged to send help, this one last time, and the message was painfully clear.

Overnight the things I could count on had all disappeared, but in time I managed to learn new skills. In the early light of morning, when the sink backed up and the toilet overflowed, I learned some pretty good tricks with a plunger. Despite the carpet that got ruined or the temper I lost, I felt proud and appeared quite the hero to Jen.

But it was hard to get used to the stranger John had become. For Jennifer's sake, I was determined to find a way to relate to this person and maintain friendly feelings between us.

When the wisteria that draped the stone walls on the drive across Central Park burst into bright yellow blossoms, we knew that another school year was nearly over. At the first sign of summer, our heavy coats were replaced by light jackets and the need for warm boots had passed. Jennifer showed a cranky side that I had not seen before, and she had been acting out with little bursts of temper. We needed a change of scene. With John's help and an airfare war, I made reservations to visit Johnny.

Soon after the semester ended, we landed in Los Angeles and Johnny was there to meet us. He wore a fine beard and mustache and it appeared that my son was no longer a boy. I was nourished by the happy faces of loved ones and all of the "secret" plans to celebrate my summer birthday. I tried to draw Jen into the spirit of fun but she just seemed unable to overcome an underlying moodiness.

Friends and family suggested that maybe she was expressing a hidden resentment toward me. Johnny said she hadn't mentioned the "half" thing but we all wondered if somehow, in her child's mind, she was blaming me for the divorce. Molly suggested that it might help if Jen realized how difficult things had been when she was too young to remember, and that if her mom had wanted to leave her dad, it would have been then. My sister Joan told her that my intention had always been, at all cost, to keep the family together and added, "Try not to be mad at your mother." Jen said, "I know," then ran off to play with Aunt Joan's dog.

A follow-up conversation with Lynn Savalas helped me decide to do something I hadn't wanted to do. Lynn also suspected that this behavior was probably anger at me for "causing" the divorce. She asked if Jen knew about the other woman, and then suggested it was time to tell her the truth. Since Jen's godmother had been there herself, I listened carefully and was grateful for her sincere wish to help. It did make sense that Jen would feel confused to have her father suddenly disappear one day when our family life had been so happy. After thinking it over, I decided to gently let her know.

When I told Jennifer this grown-up news, it was interesting to see her reaction. She remembered meeting that lady and it took several minutes for reality to sink in. Then I saw understanding wash over her face, and I knew it was the same sensation that hearing the truth often brought to me.

My sister Joan baked a cake and threw a party for my birthday. Molly wanted me to celebrate with her family, too. Her teenage daughter, Carrie (named after the first film Bill had made as a young actor), baked a carrot cake, my favorite, while Molly cooked a pork tenderloin roast for dinner. Both of my kids were again invited, and I felt well celebrated that year. Before long it was time to go home. But Jennifer was still fighting anger, though she tried her best to be cheerful. I wondered if something deep inside was changing.

When we returned to New York, she asked her father if it was true and though I never knew just what was said, it was a definite turning point. The couple came out of the closet and Jennifer began having visits with the two of them. She was growing up and rolling with the punches.

Eventually, John took Jenny to visit Yaya with his girlfriend. I thought it was too soon and a poor example, but I feared that my intervention would only add to the stress Jennifer was under. He was her father and in this case his judgment would have to do.

After one of those weekends, Jenny came home unusually troubled. She confessed that she was upset by something that happened at Yaya's. She'd been napping on the living-room couch and awoke to see her father removing photos of me. She was told that his girlfriend was sitting outside in the car and wouldn't come in until every picture of me was gone. Jen watched her father, who had always been loving and protective of me as her mother, remove my image from sight.

It took effort to hide my true feelings as I wondered what I should say. I managed to come up with the heartfelt conviction that her father had never been like that and some pressure must have caused him to behave in an unnatural way. I said that Yaya probably didn't like having her things removed either, but if she could accept it, so could we. On our very next visit the photos of me were all gone. I told Jennifer that I knew Yaya still loved me.

But when the evil "Temptress" within whispered a call to get even, I asked for guidance and managed to deafen my ear. I'd studied spiritual wisdom for too many years to ignore its guiding principles now. In the years to come my adherence to those principles was going to be tested many times.

It wasn't long before I was tempted again.

Fairy tale acting in school now culminated with a performance on the auditorium stage. It didn't matter to Jennifer that she wasn't the princess but only a flower that bent in the wind. It was a big enough worry to bend only when the "wind kids" moved across the stage. To actually be on a stage was excitement enough. "Mom, do you think Daddy will come?"

I arrived early to get a good seat, happy that Dad had said he'd come. The closed curtain began to move a little and soon Jenny's face peeked out and nervously scanned the room. When she saw me sitting there a big smile appeared and a little arm reached out to wave. I waved back discreetly and felt my throat constrict as Jenny's eyes continued to scan the room, then disappeared behind the closed curtain. When the seats were filled and it was time to begin, she took one last look and flashed me another quick smile. After the bows were all taken, she ran to me with what I already knew. "Daddy didn't come," she said. I told her she was a perfect flower, and that he was probably busy and to wait until next time. "We'll ask him to come again," I said.

It turned out that this scene was repeated many times. When her head popped out of the curtains, with those same hopeful eyes anxiously scanning the room, I'd be sure to have a tissue nearby. It was always the same. The next day I'd call her father to say that his absence had broken her heart and the response was always, "Oh. I forgot."

"But I'm afraid she might think you don't love her."

"You don't know what you're talking about. She knows I love her." I ignored the unpleasant tone.

He still never came. I really resented being put in the position of trying to make him do anything again. The battles were hard won to stay friendly. What I really wanted to do was to nail his lips to the rail road tracks so he couldn't promise her again. But I had read too many times in the spiritual books I studied that the one who knows better must do better or nothing has really sunk in.

A continuing volley of disappointments with John kept me running from one feeling to another and my mind was straining to keep up. The guy who had been sending those mushy birthday cards and romantic valentines was behaving as if he had no confidence in my judgment. I was the enemy. We were parents to the same child and there would always be things to handle together, yet this behavior was making everything more difficult. But I didn't want to parent alone so I fought to hang on to a one-sided relationship, which was all that was possible then.

One day John broached the subject of divorce again. I still didn't want one but I knew it was time to give in. I agreed with his reasoning that because of our "friendship" we could work things out without expensive lawyers or divorce court and that he'd rather give "it" to me than to the government. That was a comfort to hear. Negotiations began.

166

I was sure he'd feel that I was entitled to a good share of future earnings since he, more than anyone, knew that I was the motivating force that got him working. The mind numbing news was that he didn't remember it that way. I mentioned that it had been my idea, as well as my money, that had done the makeover to his appearance. When no response was forthcoming, I talked about buying our house and fixing it up, medical school, and the move to Greece that ended with the job in New York—all my doing. I was overcome by incredulity when his words broke the silence, "I only did those things to please you!"

"John, a well-paid manager wouldn't have done as much!" He knew that an agent lacks the skill to give input to help a career, but chose to ignore the inference.

In that usual calm way, he replied, "Now it's your turn to get a career."

"Isn't it your turn to help me?"

When he told me he'd already done all he was going to do for me, I knew our talks had ended that day. We were on opposite ends of the same issue and needed more time to think.

There was a lot to think about. In my heart I knew that no professional manager would allow him to legally walk off with all of the gains. No judge would question entitlement. Now here I was, not only without legal support but without moral support from my culture. I thought of the many women who had been left after years of helping their men through medical or law school, with the same personal deficit remaining, only to find that the role of "wife" gave a husband the advantage.

I started feeling pretty foolish for having devoted my career-building years to John's, because my security—health insurance, retirement, what I needed to raise our child, and so on—was all tied up with his. It was scary. Verbal wrangling continued until it was clear that my words were falling on deaf ears. When he said, "I'm not going to pay for this marriage the rest of my life," I almost lost it. It was pretty obvious just who would be paying the rest of whose life. My friends in California were sending fervent messages that, although John was entitled to get a divorce, I mustn't let him leave me and Jennifer stranded.

The women's movement was gaining steam and the male-dominated courts were using its verbiage to be even more heartless to displaced home managers. John kept the pressure on and with my migraine headaches becoming more debilitating, I finally agreed to far less than what I thought was fair, but to John, it was more than he wanted to pay. I was to receive a pittance each month until his yearly raise kicked in, at which time the amount would increase by a designated percent of his raise, until my support payment reached a specified sum. It was a feeble gesture designed to compensate for the fact that John left just as our finances were beginning to improve. Our only property asset was the half shares we owned in the restaurant. We divided the shares equally. I knew that it hadn't yet made a profit, but the belief that one day it would brought a modicum sense of security. In the meantime, the support payments would provide enough for Jen and me to subsist on. It would probably be a long time before my financial worries would end. When the agreement was signed, there was nothing to do but accept it and the resentment as part of the mix.

It took two years before I could say with certainty that I had a firm grip on my sanity. But in the process of recovery I had discovered that one of the great adages of history was true: time really does help heal wounds. One day I realized that the pain had settled into a manageable part of my psyche and I could actually move on.

Chapter 12
BEGINNING AGAIN

S TARTING OVER IN MIDDLE AGE wouldn't be easy and there was still eleven-year-old Jennifer to raise. I wanted to find a job that fit my talent and interests, both of which had centered on family for so many years. I considered acting again, but the worship of youth and constant rejection built into that business might prove too risky for my bruised ego and tenuous emotional state. I needed to find something more stable.

I felt like a child with no past, wondering what to do about my future. After a few months of counseling with Barbara Callen, my therapist, I discovered that I actually had good insights and instinctively understood how to apply her analytical concepts. She noticed it, too, and suggested that I might want to consider psychology as a profession. It would be a chance to help others as well as to earn a living. I gave it some thought. Friends did often come to me with their problems and I enjoyed being there for them. Her suggestion was good. I had always wanted to finish college; maybe it wasn't too late. I hopped on a bus to Hunter College to see if I had any credits to apply toward a degree in psychology. I had enough to enter as a Junior. Very encouraging.

A second possibility arose when I thought about my long-standing interest in natural healing methods. In my early twenties, severe migraine headaches began to darken several days a month and my doctor said there was no cure. So I began to study health and nutrition. I found some relief for myself and often used this knowledge to help my children and friends. Perhaps I could apply all those years of study and do something in the field of nutritional therapy. What credentials would I need? I'd heard about a school in Manhattan that taught medical massage. Accredited by the Board of Education, its graduates receive a New York State license to practice. I paid a visit there and it, too, looked promising. Neither school started classes until fall, so there was plenty of time to make a choice.

The monthly pittance from John hadn't increased and the restaurant wasn't making a profit, so financial worries and fear about my security still hadn't let up. The fact that I would begin classes in the fall for a new profession helped ease the pressure. I would soon have a career and when the restaurant started making a profit, my finances would be in good order. The future looked promising. With careful budgeting, Jen and I would manage until then.

Drained from hammering out the divorce and with another summer fast approaching, I decided to recuperate on the West Coast. I knew at this point in my life it was important to make the right decision about school. John agreed to buy a ticket for Jen and soon we were boarding the plane.

170

As we prepared for landing, there was the usual rush of good feelings knowing that Johnny was down there waiting. The mere presence of that young man was healing for me. Jen was full of news and questions on the long drive to the valley. A year of catching up filled each silent moment and it was hard to get a word in with those two.

It was wonderful to inhale the familiar air of Johnny's apartment. I was happy to have both of my children with me again. Johnny proudly showed us his new electric guitar. It was a recent purchase and his most cherished possession. He explained that it took a lot of hard work and sacrifice to buy such a fine instrument and warned his sister never to touch it. None of us had the money to buy another and if it got broken there would be real hell to pay. The warning was so stern that even I was afraid to go near it.

It was hot and smoggy and the valley was sizzling. Potato salad and cold cuts had been a favorite on summer days. I said, "Jen let's go to the store and surprise Johnny when he comes home from work." She preferred to stay home, saying, "It's so boring at the store and more fun to watch TV."

I'd been trying to be less protective and to give her more freedom, so I let her stay home. I returned a little while later and was stunned by the sight of my daughter sitting on the couch, holding in each naughty hand one half of Johnny's precious guitar. It was broken in two, strings dangling free. The force of anger raged in my voice as I asked for an explanation. She'd been pretending to play when it slipped to the floor and snapped at the neck into two useless pieces.

A monster took hold of my senses. I yelled at and badgered Jen for touching the one thing that was strictly off limits. "How will we ever replace it? We used all our money to pay for this trip

171

and school takes most of Johnny's. He is going to be furious that his warning was ignored! What can I do?" This hysterical woman ranted on for some time but finally calmed down to wait for Johnny to come home.

It was an eternity before he appeared and Jennifer bolted for the bedroom. I delivered the news right away, before he had a chance to see his most valued possession broken in two. In a calm, reassuring tone I asked that he please not be mad at Jen, and added with knowing sincerity that she's been through enough. I agreed to pay to have it fixed or buy a new one.

To my great relief and surprise, he called her to come out and said, "C'mon babe, let's go get it fixed." That's all that was said as they picked up the pieces and went out the door. Wow, that's not the reaction I expected! Had my son developed a fine sense of compassion? The guitar was fixed by a master to look like new. It took me forever to pay the bill, but I wished I hadn't lost my temper with Jen.

Jen regained her old cheerfulness and the summer turned out to be the medicine both of us needed, though the guitar incident made staying home alone less appealing to her. After a month in the sun, I made my decision about school and we returned to New York.

A fat letter from John's attorney stood out from the rest and in it was my final divorce decree. The papers shook in my hands as I read right there in black and white that a large part of my life was over. Tears filled my eyes and pressure gripped my throat. I quickly scanned the page. There was a line that asked for the number of "issues" in the marriage and someone had typed in "one." She's not an "issue!" Her name is Jennifer, I bawled out loud and let the paper drop to the floor. The loving, living, breathing little girl who had brought so much joy to our marriage was now just another one of the above-mentioned items to which I was given full custody.

As my tears subsided, the photographs adorning the old secondhand piano came into view. I had spent many happy hours trimming pictures of my family to fit those odd-sized antique frames. My gaze fell on one that I took of Jen and her dad before we left California. It had been one of our favorites. I had captured them both with the same pouting expression looking straight into the camera. My gaze wandered from shot to shot, moments captured on film when our family was happy. What will I do with them now? I guess I should take them down. But how would Jen feel if familiar images of her family were no longer there? It didn't take long to decide what to do. I would not only keep those pictures but I would go through the ones in that big box and make a wonderful gallery to line the hall. Each morning when Jen leaves her room she'll be reminded that all of us love her.

I wiped the last tear, then said to my tan face in the mirror, "It's time to register at Hunter College." I opted for a chance to graduate college and resurrect one of my dreams. Yes, Hunter would be the right choice. I phoned the office and heard the terrible news that admission tests had been given the previous week and I would have to wait until next year.

It was impossible. I didn't have another year. So I enrolled in that medical massage course and began a very intensive year of study. In addition to practical technique, I would study the entire human body and all of its parts. Hours of memorizing would be required, and in order to get the license there were State Boards to pass. It seemed promising. Fate prevented college but I chose to believe it was for the best. The start of a migraine caused a resurgence of doubt. Could I carry this load? Then I forced the panic to leave.

There was just enough time before school began to decorate my bedroom with some lovely old pieces I'd taken out of storage to ship from California that summer. I wanted our home to be inviting and beautiful as everything fell into place.

Jennifer was anxious to return to school and amused by the idea that we would both have homework now. According to my schedule, all of my classes were in the morning and I finished by one o'clock, which left a couple of hours for study before it was time to pick up Jen. A turn-of-the-century dresser and chest (another find from those treasure hunting days), a gallon of paint, and Susan's help making curtains did wonders for my bedroom. Jen and I both had back-to-school jitters when it was time for school to begin. From the first day I liked the atmosphere of learning. Jen, happy to be reunited with her friends, had a lot to talk about at dinner.

There was a new boy in Jennifer's class and all of the girls fell in love. He wore leather wristbands, walked with a swagger, and was the first "cool" guy they'd ever seen. During the first few weeks of school, Jennifer came home each day with a different name of just which girl loved him the most. As one lovestruck girl after another came forth with their admission, the count grew to an unmanageable number. It all came to a resolution when the boy agreed to pick one girl to love back. Just who it was remained a mystery for another few weeks as the boy basked in the attention. Each day Jen was a little more impatient and eager to be the one.

One day she told me that tomorrow the big winner would be announced. The girls had all ganged up and forced him to reveal the lucky girl's name. Jenny's eyes shined with anticipation. That's all we talked about through dinner and on the ride to school the next morning. When I dropped her off, I wished her the best and was surprised to find how much I wanted for her to be the one. She arrived home that day with a very sad face and said that another girl had been chosen. My heart broke right along with hers as I fumbled for the right words to say. Then her expression changed and she said an extraordinary thing. The lucky girl was her best friend and Jen could imagine how happy she must be! I was amazed to see that the happiness of a friend had assuaged my daughter's disappointment. I liked the character she displayed!

Life was becoming more stable and, like most women in those days, mine had centered around family; because of this, New York friends had mostly come through John's work. It was of ongoing interest for me to figure out which of us got custody of which friend. I still preferred to stay home or go places with Jen. My preference gained added emphasis when Jen burst into the house and said she hated one of our doormen. She said he'd taken her to a secluded part of our building and had shown her a magazine full of pornographic pictures while asking, "What do you think of that?" She was upset and quite frightened. For a moment I was too stunned to know what to do. The man who was paid to protect us had intruded on my child's innocence. I told John and he immediately contacted the superintendent of our building who said there was nothing he could do since the man hadn't left his post! (We learned that "post" meant the entire building.) It was torment for both Jen and me when we encountered him during his shift. It was a huge relief when a few weeks later he just vanished. He later reappeared, but never went near Jen or worked in our building again.

I interpreted the experience to be a reminder that life in

175

Manhattan could sometimes be dangerous and certain restrictions were needed. I was more determined than ever to be home when Jen wasn't in school or at the house of a friend. But when Jen wasn't home, I never felt quite at ease.

Anatomy; biology; cytology; embryology; pathology; nervous, venous, and lymph systems; and more faced me at school. There were hours of intense study. I organized sessions at my house with Rachel and Doris, two nice women from class. They said I should get out and have more fun. My initial resistance was finally overcome when Jen visited her father one weekend, and Rachel convinced me to go to a party. It was there that I met a man who became my first romantic encounter in what seemed like a hundred years since I met John. It felt strange at first.

Sam Hitz was several years younger but really quite interesting and I found it attractive when he dazzled me with his boyish charms. He said I was irresistibly enchanting. Jennifer liked him, too. Before long we were all going out to dinner. One night Jen was gone and we were alone in my kitchen when mutual desire was exchanged in our first passionate kiss. For some unknown reason, right in the middle, I started to giggle. Sam was a large man who suddenly seemed even larger when he pulled away angrily. I tried to explain, "I'm sorry. You see, I was married a long time and haven't dated in years." I wanted to resume our passion but with each attempt the giggles started again. As hard as I tried not to, I would burst into laughter again. He was understandably offended, but the funny bug had taken a big bite. Short shrift was made of that kiss and he decided to leave. The next day I sent an apology with a single red rose. Our attraction was strong and we were soon dating again.

I was surprised when Jen mentioned that Sam might dress a

176

little nicer. I thought he looked fine. Then she said he burped during a meal and eventually her dislike grew to loathing. The complaining increased to a daily reminder that "You could do better Mom." It was a clear indication that she wasn't ever going to accept Sam. My priority was Jen, so I ended the relationship.

"Great Mom, you're too beautiful for that guy and thank God we don't ever have to see him again."

John was living with his girlfriend and decided that Jennifer would spend weekends with them. With this decision I worried less about her missing her dad. It came as a complete surprise when she began returning home as sad and as troubled as ever. I tried to find out what was wrong but she insisted it was nothing. I was even more confused when she tried to describe incidents she only half understood. I never knew quite what to say so I suggested she talk to her father. But she said that was too scary.

After one of those weekend visits, she flopped in a chair and complained, "They're going to make me see a shrink to help me adjust." I told her it might be a chance to tell her father what she had been too scared to say. I convinced her to give it a try and an appointment was made for later in the week.

After the appointment, she walked through the door and said it was worse than awful and headed straight for her room, refusing to say another word except that she would never ever go there again.

Winter came fast in 1980, and before long we'd had another wonderful Christmas. The very next day Jennifer went with her dad for a week of family celebrations. My friend Rachel from school talked me into going to a New Year's Eve party at the home of a woman I didn't know. Rachel thought I would find the woman interesting because she was a therapist who specialized

177

in stepparent counseling and would have many fascinating stories to tell.

The woman was proud of some books that she'd written on stepparenting and showed us the room where they were on display. It wasn't long before I realized that her method didn't favor the child. It wasn't my thing so I paid very little attention, but felt somehow encouraged about my own future plans.

It was a decent party, but I really preferred to be at home. I stayed just to be polite. When it was finally time for us to walk the few short blocks home, the cold winter air felt invigorating on my face. Rachel asked me what I had thought of our host. She then said I could learn a lot from that woman because after a difficult divorce she had come a long way. She had been trying to get a writing career off the ground when she married a man with children. It was a bad experience that led to divorce and to a career as a stepparent therapist! Rachel laughed with admiration as she recalled that the woman often boasted about turning a bad experience into good. I took encouragement from that.

Finals were approaching so my study group met more often. Everyone passed. We then began an even more intensive study for the State Boards. Hours of memorizing were making us crazy. When the day finally arrived to take our exams, it was a relief to walk into that large, crowded room full of strangers and know it would soon be over. One by one we finished and left the test area to wait each day for the mail. When the news arrived, I was amazed and terribly pleased to find I'd not only passed but had scored a very high grade.

I bought a massage table, opened a practice, and waited for the first customer to answer my ad. It soon became apparent that massage therapy hadn't caught on in New York. Not one client came. More waiting. To improve our skills Rachel, Doris, and I practiced on each other. In the process a terrible discovery was made: I simply didn't have enough strength to do a full hour of massage. In school we learned the technique one stoke at a time and I hadn't realized how much energy a whole session takes. There was no getting around it, massage would take more strength than I had. Therapeutic massage was not for me. I convinced myself that it didn't matter, that the experience and knowledge was worth the investment, but it was clearly back to square one. After nearly two years of study and the high cost of the course, I hadn't the time or the money to go back to college.

There was talk of a new method of counseling that people learn to do in private homes. It's based on the premise that incidents causing emotional pain are often experienced at a lower level of emotional development; returning to the incident with maturity can bring new insights and healing. People meet in private homes to reevaluate each other as a volunteer teaches the technique. The fee was minimal, covering costs and refreshments. I reasoned that if I found this method to be effective, I could limit my practice to medical massage and counsel with the same license. I decided to give it a try. Everyone there took turns being therapist or patient. I soon learned that a lot of casting blame was going on. The objective sharing of responsibility that Barbara Callen had so painstakingly guided me through was lacking. I was exchanging counseling with a young woman and after some time I noticed that her problems just wouldn't leave my mind. My own emotional state was further disturbed. I needed more healing before I could help others. For now, the job of a therapist wasn't for me either.

Rachel and Doris were also having a tough time getting their massage practices off the ground. There were plenty of people willing to offer their bodies for practice and some even paid a few dollars, but my friends had little need for their state license and mine hung unused on my wall.

A stockbroker was going to give a talk at the 92nd St. Y on improving one's financial picture. It sounded like something I sorely needed so I talked Rachel into going with me. We arrived early to get a seat in the front row so I would hear every word. Out of the corner of my eye, I noticed a man sitting in the seat next to mine. When I turned to get a better look, I couldn't move my gaze from his warm brown eyes. His well-chiseled face softened with admiration as he searched the counters of mine. A dazzling smile of white teeth and dimples (almost unexpected in that rugged face) suggested a sense of fun I wanted to know.

"Hi, my name is Lawrence Levine," he said.

In the next moment our eyes held as we gazed through the door to each other's soul. It was impossible to concentrate when the lecture began. I didn't hear a word. When it was over, he asked for my phone number; without hesitation, I complied.

To enter the unfamiliar world of another, who pleased me in so many ways, brought to life feelings I thought were gone forever. A tall, slender professor, with brown, curly hair, Larry taught science courses at Columbia University. His voice was soft, yet confident when he spoke. He told me about his difficult childhood and painful divorce. A few years younger than me, his understanding contained the wisdom of a very old man.

Larry caressed me with an intimacy I had never known as his tender words touched my soul. He worshiped at the altar of this new love.

When I told him of my need to get a job he said he'd always

wanted to start a small business and that since his job only required part-time hours, we could start one together. It was an unexpected bonus to have a man at my side in this way. We found a product to sell and set out in the morning to call on customers until noon. Then we dropped into a charming place that served a fabulous fish for lunch and told each other stories about customers we'd just seen.

Jennifer adored him, too.

It was encouraging to have someone in my corner sharing happy times as well as the frustrations of divorce. He had a sympathetic ear and helpful advice of all kinds, which encouraged me to seek his counsel with the long, dreary tale of my marriage. He listened as I recounted incidents of all I had done, while asking nothing for myself, and I ended with how I had even protected John's new-found success from being spoiled by grieving for my mother's death. I settled back to receive the expected, "How could he leave such a woman?" With an expression that said "are you from another planet," he replied with incredulity, "John didn't need that!"

"What are you trying to say?"

"Some men get lost in external matters and pay little attention to feelings like grief." It wasn't the reaction I expected. It didn't even make sense at the time, but I often wondered if his inference was that John's only concern was to work as an actor and not about me. Larry wasn't usually that unkind.

As Lawrence felt more comfortable and at home with me, he began to change. When my Adonis noticed other men looking at me, his adoring admiration turned to criticism and withholding of affection. His jealousy, at first subtle and a little flattering, soon became ugly accusations that spoiled every moment we shared. I tried to be understanding because, as an insecure teenage bride I, too, had bouts of uncontrolled jealousy and knew how painful it could be. The more tolerant I was, the more out of control he became. If I accidentally looked in the direction of another man, he disappeared into a sulk that lasted for days. Even Jen said she could see it was hopeless. My feelings began to change.

The relationship lasted for more than a year, long beyond the limits of normal tolerance. Being left for another woman had so pitifully deflated my ego that I was afraid to let him go. I knew it would be a long time before I would take another gamble on love.

After visits with her father, Jennifer was still coming home unhappy and still couldn't explain to me why. When she started acting out in school, I tried talking to John but received a surprising "Hell-hath-no-fury-like-a-woman-scorned speech." My concerns were perceived as mere distortions of a typical scorned woman! The two people who needed to pull together to raise our daughter were split by a shallow cliché.

Jennifer and I were in the kitchen talking, paying little attention to what was coming from a nearby television. A pause in our conversation allowed us to hear a talk-show host announce that the next guest was an authority on stepparenting. Our attention was riveted to a woman's voice saying that children can ruin their parent's lives. As if it happened on cue, we both dashed to the set and Jennifer said, "Oh my god, that's the shrink they made me see." I told Jen that I had spent last New Year's Eve at her home. We stood there transfixed as the woman explained that often a divorce turns kids into manipulative little monsters. She offered, with great authority, that they will try anything to get their birth parents back together and a good second marriage can be ruined if a smart couple doesn't put the stepparent's concerns first and refuse to give in to their children's demands. After all, they'll grow up and be gone some day and one must protect what one has.

Wow! I was right; that woman doesn't favor kids. Now I understood what Jennifer couldn't put into words and why that therapist had such a big following. With the number of divorces and stepparenting on the rise, it seemed to me that she gave just what stepparents wanted—permission to relegate another woman's child, who should have come first, to second-string status. Poor Jenny couldn't understand and was finding it impossible to cope. She didn't stand a chance in that carefully laid plan.

When I told John, he once again responded with the hell-hath-no-fury theory, and his willingness to doubt my motives told me that we would no longer be united for our daughter. The voice of my cynical culture and another woman had replaced cooperation between us. It was pure hell.

I had to confess to Jennifer that therapy isn't always good and that there was no hope of my changing the situation at Dad's. I suggested she come to me if things got too difficult, because I would be there to help. This started a process that brought us even closer as Jen frequently found occasions to ask for that help. Sometimes I just held her.

My once promising romance was now history, along with the small business. I had to find work. I heard some vague talk about our restaurant being too much for John to handle, so again I volunteered to work there. But again he told me no. I argued the importance of that business to Jen's and my future security and emphasized my willingness to handle the work and still be home when Jen needed me. That reasoning also ended with a negative response.

A few weeks later, John telephoned to say that there was

serious trouble at the restaurant and it had to be sold. He must have my half of our shares. I pleaded, "No, don't sell my security. I can get it out of trouble. Please."

"It can't be done," he said. "We'll get fifty thousand dollars and you can have it all."

"Please, John, no, let me save the restaurant, I can't let it go!"

"Nancy, the restaurant can't be saved! The papers have been signed and to back out now would cause serious trouble for everyone, maybe even Jen."

That's all I needed to hear. He came right over to pick up my shares. I waited for a long time but the fifty thousand dollars never came.

"There was no money," he said without blinking an eye. "Just be happy we're out of that mess."

My future security was gone.

Chapter 13

YOU'RE ALWAYS WELCOME HERE

DIVORCE MEANT GETTING USED TO the way things were going to be.

One day, I was inadvertently reminded of an unhealed wound in my heart. Jen came home from a visit with her father and excitedly told me that Dad had bought a house in the country. The purchase of that house was a reminder that we had sold our home in California to finance four years of medical school in Greece. After the sale, John had promised to replace it with a better one someday—that day would never come. I was feeling irritated by the injustice until Jenny said, "Mom, their house is in ski country and Dad's going to let me take lessons." That would be a good thing for Jennifer, which is always a good thing for me. My irritation became just another broken promise to remove from my craw.

Jen was a natural skier. She sailed through the basics right into the advanced class, and soon she was skiing down high mountains. She was coming home happy. "Dad's friends say my skiing is very good, too!"

When perfect conditions led to extra long hours of skiing, Jen strained her body to the limit. Every muscle burned with pain. She limped into her room and asked if I thought she was permanently damaged and if it was really worth it.

"Of course it is. Don't forget I give a good massage. We'll get rid of that pain."

She flinched, "Oooh, don't touch me."

I said, "C'mon," as I set up the padded table. In an hour and a half I slowly worked out all of the pain.

"Mommy, this is amazing. Can you teach me how? Daddy has terrible backaches and this massage thing is just what he needs." So I taught her how to give a dynamite back rub, and the new skill helped her Dad more than anyone expected. Jen was ecstatic with pride. But it wasn't going to last long.

Several weeks later, another weekend was over and Jennifer came home overwhelmed and distraught. It was obvious that something hurtful had happened. She was only thirteen, very upset, and didn't really completely understand. But I gathered that all physical contact with her father must stop. She said her dad and his girlfriend had spoken with her about "a matter of great importance." She was told something to the effect that as little girls grow up, ordinary affection for a father may lead to an unhealthy attraction. From now on all hugging and kissing and especially those back rubs must stop.

"I'm so sorry" was all I could say. It looked like manipulating Jen out of her Dad's life had been raised to an art. Though physically there, she'd been removed on the emotional level. This "scorned woman" knew it was pointless to say a word.

Jen asked, "Is it true?"

"I suppose, in some rare cases," I said. "But in your case Daddy is wrong." I added, "Don't think he doesn't love you because he's made a mistake." I then asked her to be patient again.

But my patience was running out and I secretly wanted never to see John again. It wasn't easy, but for the sake of my child I managed to stay friendly.

Jen had always loved to jump into her father's arms when he came home or cuddle close to him on the couch. With the no-touching rule being strictly enforced, it must have seemed to her that when he was there he really wasn't. I couldn't bear to think of her standing near him, unable to show physical affection. The result may have been that she started missing him again. Her feelings surfaced one day after school.

She burst into the room, tossed her books on a chair, fell back against the door, and exhaling, said that her friend Mary was so lucky. She had watched Mary's father arrive at school to plant kisses all over his daughter's giggling face, then squeeze her in a really big hug. "Mommy, I stood there watching and wished my daddy loved me like that."

"Darling, I know he does." I told her that a long time ago, her father and I left a party early because we missed her and came home just to watch her sleeping. I went on to say that as we stood gazing into her crib, I saw Daddy's love shining out of his face and I knew it was still there. Once again I asked that she be patient, but by now my words sounded empty.

Jen began doing poorly in school.

With money so short, I really needed a job and put the word

out to some of my friends. So far nothing looked very promising. It was puzzling. I had found my first job at just thirteen and was frustrated to find it so difficult now that I had so much life experience behind me. I wondered if I was encountering age discrimination or perhaps my problem was wanting part-time work. But I wasn't going to let Jen come home to an empty house. There must be something that fit my needs. The search continued.

During years of volunteer work for a spiritual movement, a friend admired my managerial skills and had also commented that I wrote exceptionally good letters. I appreciated Beth's efforts to help because she had spent many years in the business world and I valued her advice.

One day she approached me with an unusually good offer. A high-profile man Beth met through business needed an assistant to keep his life running smoothly. Respect for her opinion prompted this man to ask if she knew someone to recommend for the job. It appeared Beth was recommending me. The date and time for the interview was set and as I dressed for the appointment, I found my hand shaking.

I arrived at an elegant fifth avenue building and had just enough time to check my hair in the lobby mirror. Then it was time to go up. Heart, don't betray me now, I prayed with each knock on the door, but it just pounded harder. I really wanted the job. The door opened to a spacious entry filled with stunning antiques. The man had excellent taste. A maid ushered me into the study where, sitting at an eighteenth-century desk, was one of the handsomest men I'd ever seen. I tried not to stammer or blush. Relax, I told myself, be casual.

He told me that the job included managing and staffing his household, but what he needed most was someone to make travel and lodging arrangements and to organize his overcrowded appointment schedule. The traveling could get extensive at times and would involve a daily rash of meetings, and he'd need whoever took the job to go with him on those trips.

I had always planned to travel and this news was a dream coming true. For a split second I thought of the places we might go, but then I realized that it was impossible.

He was saying that the pay would be good because he needed total dedication and the hours at times would be long. He asked when I could start.

"Couldn't you use someone part time? You see, I have a child who is too young to be left home alone." Of course part time was out of the question. I had to turn down the best job offer I ever had. The timing was lousy.

Beth said I had made the right decision because the reports from Jen's school still weren't good. Homework and study was increasingly demanding, but Jen was more interested in socializing and wouldn't stop talking in class. I promised the teacher she'd do better but, except for play acting, friends, and excursions, she was not liking school.

I tried to assuage my worry with the fact that the Rudolf Steiner School was a familiar haven that Jennifer returned to everyday. If she needed to act out, it was good that it happened there. The school's policy of having the same class teacher every day for the first eight years turns the teacher into something like another parent and the children become more like brothers and sisters who feel less of a separation from home. The school's view is that each child has his or her own special destiny and is treated with respect for their personal uniqueness in an atmosphere that feels like home. Jennifer's artistic nature was allowed to thrive and her special qualities went undisturbed. If she was going to do poorly in that wonderful school, I was sure that she would have fared much worse in another school system.

I will always be grateful to John for agreeing to pay Jennifer's tuition, because it brought stability to her life and made up for a lot that was lacking. To change might have brought disaster.

Life wasn't perfect but it never is, and John's generosity with the tuition helped mitigate the fallout from our divorce. Jen and I did a pretty good job making things okay and always found something to laugh about.

In New York City, from the richest to the poorest, everyone has a problem with cockroaches. They multiply in staggering numbers and arrive in a variety of sizes. One night around three in the morning, I awoke to visit the loo. Sitting there with eyes half closed, glancing at the sink, I wondered what that big brown animal was. Standing there, at just my eye level, with tentacles slowly moving, was the ugliest bug God ever created. I let out a blood-curdling shriek and, without lifting my undies, stumbled straight to Jennifer's room, falling hard against the door. She woke with a start and asked what all the noise was about. I explained that a bug, more ugly than Satan, was making our bathroom his home. Knowing how much I hated such critters, Jennifer jumped up to help and together we went to show him the door. We held onto each other as I flicked him from the sink toward the toilet, but that lucky sucker missed the bowl completely and fell to the floor. We screamed out with fright and made a mad dash for the door, then gathered our courage to creep carefully back. We found him in a corner behind the commode. I pulled up the carpet, ran to the kitchen, and brought back the bug spray. I sprayed until he was almost submerged in a milky white pool. He became very still.

Wanting to be absolutely sure that the liquid had taken effect, we decided to wait it out in the living room. We said to each other that neither of us had ever seen a bug that big. Half an hour later we returned to dispose of the corpse. He certainly looked dead to me. With a hand full of paper, I reached for his carcass to toss in the toilet for flushing. I had barely touched that still body when he shot out like a race horse leaving the gate and we shot in the opposite direction. A cup of poison hadn't fazed him one bit. That bug was the size of a child's pet gerbil and there'd be no sleeping with it in the house.

We were tossing around ideas of what to do next. I saw an empty toilet paper roll in the trash and got an idea. I ran for a baggy and attached it to one end of the roll and by placing it in front of the path he was taking, invited the bug to enter. He ran straight to Momma and I quickly twisted the open end and together we marched to the trash shoot. With the spoils of our victory extended way out in front, we sighed with relief that the crisis was over.

We told the story on our next visit to Yaya's and she knew the bug we were talking about. From time to time she found one in the basement and warned us to be careful not to ever squash one or the whole house would fill with a terrible odor that would linger for days and days. Not for a dance with Prince Charles would we have squashed anything that big but said we were glad that we hadn't anyway.

The photos of me were still absent from Yaya's table and walls, but the connection between us remained strong. It was by chance and a happy coincidence that I often arrived when her health was ailing and could help with doctor visits and such. I've always had a soft spot for older women. I know it must be hard to age alone with your husband gone. I wanted to do whatever was possible to

191

lighten that burden for Yaya. She'd helped us during those difficult years and I was grateful for any small way to give something back.

Back home the telephone rang. "Nancy, I don't want you to go to my mother's house anymore."

The voice on the other end of the phone was familiar but what it was saying was so absurd that I questioned if it was anyone I knew. "What do you mean?" was all that came out as John said that his life would be easier if I just did what he asked.

For the sake of peace between us and Jen's well-being, I had swallowed a lot, but this latest demand was right out of left field. I put my foot down. "It's good for our daughter to be with family and my being there, too, is even better. For the first time since our divorce there'll be no compromise in this matter and nothing you say will convince me to go along with your outrageous request."

He insisted some more and repeated that it would make his life easier. I refused and stood my ground. "Why would you want to prevent the good that comes from our visits, which, by the way, make everyone else's life easier? Mom is happy because she loves the company. Jen enjoys seeing her relatives and learning Greek culture. And it's a wonderful way for us to get out of the city. No, it's out of the question. I plan to continue the visits as usual."

"Okay, then I'll have to talk to Mom."

He hung up and I could tell by the sound of his stubborn intention that he meant every word. I dropped into a chair. Mom would have to give in because he's her son and peace between them was more important. She would still have visits with Jenny, though it would be much less frequent. As much as I loved her, I was just an ex-daughter-in-law. I sat grieving the certain loss of those I regarded as family. When and how will Yaya ever tell me? I jumped every time the telephone rang.

192

When I finally heard Mom's warm, friendly voice on the phone, I braced for the news that would follow. Her words were clear and the surprise of my life when their full meaning became even clearer. "I called to tell you how much I enjoy having you in my home and we all look forward to your visits. Please know that you're always welcome here."

It was deeply touching that this lady who I called Mom had the courage and strength to go against years of tradition and do what was right. A similar call came from my sister-in-law and my respect for those two women knew no bounds. I felt proud to be part of that family and hoped that nothing would ever happen to change it.

Jenny was becoming quite a skier. My resilient thirteen-year-old daughter had adjusted to the no-touching rule and her love of the sport made visits with her dad something wonderful to look forward to. Winter was almost over and from the reports I was hearing, perfect conditions had made practice ideal.

We had to hurry to get ready that Friday because John was coming to take Jen early for what promised to be an especially good weekend. The weather reports had said the snow was perfect and skiers were heading for the mountains in droves. Jen was giddy with excitement and I was worried we'd forget to pack something. As I kissed her goodbye, it felt good to know that things had settled into a routine. It was like riding the crest of a wave. I forgot about the part of the wave that follows right behind and was crashed to the bottom again.

Jen came home crying from another weekend that started out happy. "Daddy said that from now on my weekend visits will be cut to every other week because he and his girlfriend need some weekends alone. Aren't they alone every day? I begged him,

'Please don't do that, Daddy,' but he kept saying he needed this time to be alone."

I held her real tight as she pleaded and wept on my shoulder.

"Mommy, there are just three weekends left before they close the lift. He's with her every day. Please, can you talk him into waiting till ski season is over so I can practice a little longer? I asked but he won't give in."

Jen was sobbing and I knew the issue wasn't skiing. She felt another rejection from the father she couldn't touch.

Okay "scorned woman," this time you will have to be heard! The repercussion could be too far-reaching. I was determined to change his mind. A few days later there was a meeting at Jen's school requiring his presence as well as mine and the timing was perfect. We drove there together. A bitter cold rain was coming down in buckets and when the meeting was over, we dashed to the car and sat a moment to talk.

"Yes the weekend visits will be cut to every other week," he confirmed, "because I need to have time for my relationship."

I reminded him that it had been hard for me to live with the insecurities left by rejection in my childhood and he certainly sympathized with that. But the decision had been made and nothing was going to change his mind.

"Jennifer knows I love her, but sorry, the three remaining weekends of ski season are out of the question."

Feelings of incredulity gave me the courage to ask something I'd been wondering about for months. "How can you live without her?" No response. "I can't imagine being happy if Jenny lived somewhere else."

He just blinked a rapid eye motion and kept silent, which was going to be his only reaction to my question. To keep from raking his face with my nails, I lowered my head. The torrents of water streaming down the windshield reflected a pattern on my raincoat and my tears were falling in time with the rain. It was like encountering the same level of resistance that drove me to rage in our marriage when he refused to get a job. But this time I found myself begging, "Please, she has so much to cope with, let her win just this once!" But he refused.

At home she was sleeping soundly and looked so peaceful in the shard of light from the hall. I had failed her again. I stood watching her for a long time, thinking about my own dad and wondering how I would tell her in the morning.

Jennifer got used to the alternate weekends and I got over my anger. But one thing was pretty clear: if I was going to have a friendly relationship with my ex-husband, I was going to do it alone.

Before long, spring was in the air and plans for Jenny's eighth-grade graduation were being made. In a serious tone, Jenny announced that she'd made an important decision. Hours of agonizing thought had led to this moment.

"I'm not going to invite Daddy to my graduation." Her chin quivered on the last word.

I asked, "Why not?"

"Because he won't come alone and his girlfriend's presence might spoil the day for you."

It was tempting for a moment, but this was an issue of character, so I resisted temptation and asked, "Wouldn't it be awful to graduate without Daddy there?"

"Yes, but it's my decision." Her chin was quivering again.

I asked if she remembered how badly I felt to be excluded from her cousins' weddings. Did we really want to do that to anyone?

"But Mommy, I want it to be a good day for you!"

I told her that wanting it to be a good day was enough for me, and it might spoil everything if I had to watch her graduate wishing that Daddy was there. I suggested that we invite him and see what happens. If he doesn't come alone, well, so be it. At least we would have done the right thing. We changed the subject by discussing what Jenny would wear.

John arrived on graduation day with his girlfriend and I knew the future would be full of similar situations and I had better get used to it. It was and I did. Well, sort of.

A very grown-up Jennifer accepted her diploma and I knew my baby was gone. Soon after that, she asked me to please stop calling her "baby." Hadn't she just been born?

Chapter 14
I DIDN'T HAVE THIS PROBLEM WHEN I WAS YOUNG!

N EW YORK EMPLOYERS WERE NOT accepting my offer: a strong, fortyish woman with plenty of life experience, no stranger to hard work, and willing to learn anything, was pounding the pavement but finding no takers.

"You've worked as a homemaker for how many years?"

"Your typing speed's not very good."

"Why do I have to tell you my age? Sorry."

I was simply not in demand. I needed to talk to Molly.

Her voice was sympathetic. "Try not to worry," she said.

I launched into what sounded like a long diatribe to justify my existence. "I'm sure it's my age because I didn't have this problem when I was young. Ironic. When I got my first job at the corner drugstore, I was too young and had to tell them I was older. You had to be sixteen. I really had fun serving food and meeting customers behind the lunch counter. That is, until I made the mistake of lean-ing forward to serve a customer one day as the cook passed behind and pressed himself against my rear, which I stupidly ignored."

Molly chuckled knowingly and said that fortunately times have changed.

"That old goat knew from my silence that I didn't know how to handle such things. He was right—I was just fourteen. So he started touching my posterior with that same extended member whenever he could until I finally had to quit."

Molly said she remembered a few similar experiences of her own and that it was terrible that I was the one to lose the job.

"I found a better one right away but it was too far from home," I told her. "Then I was hired to work at a movie theater near school. It was great. I saw all the latest films."

Molly said she worked as a model in high school.

"My dad wouldn't have let me," I replied. "Eventually I left that theater job for higher pay at a local Cinerama and worked there through twelfth grade. It was always easy to get a job!"

"You're still young. Don't get discouraged. You'll find one soon. Why don't you give yourself a break and come to L.A. for a few weeks?"

After we hung up, I remembered that there wasn't much time to be a kid when I was growing up, but I didn't much like being one anyway.

It was hard to accept that so many years later, with more life experience and capabilities, I was finding it impossible to land a job. Even when my first husband's work had us traveling around the country, I took a modeling course and worked in many cities. When that marriage ended, I taught modeling. Stop thinking about the past, Nancy. Yes, please.

198

But I couldn't stop. *Two marriages, struggle, divorce, more struggle. If it's the last thing I do, Jen's life will be easier than mine!*

It was impossible not to get discouraged because it was more than twenty years since I had worked in an office, and one after another the interviewers continued to turn me down. That damned experience. I knew I could please one of them with my ability to work hard if given the chance.

Jennifer graduated from eighth grade and John again provided her ticket for a much needed trip to the coast. Our suitcases were all packed for a month in California with my son. Out of nowhere, a friend asked if I still needed a job. I didn't walk but ran to the interview. The company was located in the Chrysler building. I felt a moment of relief that I'd overcome my fear of heights because the beautifully decorated offices were located on the sixtieth floor. The business was advertising where people skills and appearance are important and mine on both counts were good. But my typing was pretty embarrassing.

Betty Parker, my future boss, said it didn't matter because it was more important to find someone responsible to fill in at the reception desk. Almost everything comes and goes through that spot and it was crucial to find a dependable person who could handle several problems at once. I said it sounded like being a wife and mother, for which I had many years of on-the-job experience. I met all the requirements and Betty said the typing in time would improve. The hours were pretty flexible and she wanted to know how soon I could start. Remembering our packed suitcases at home, I said, "In a month." We compromised and shook hands on three weeks.

A job at last! With that happy news Jennifer and I took off for Kennedy Airport, giddy with excitement. I handed the skycap a camera to take our picture as the driver removed luggage from the cab. Before long it was time to board and we found seats in the smoking section at the rear. There was the usual scolding from Jen to quit smoking. People were beginning to suspect that second-hand smoke might cause health problems, but flying really made me nervous. I said, "I know. Soon, Honey."

We talked about my new job while the plane took off and the tilt threw us back in our seats. Jennifer wanted to know what it's like to work in an office, to answer phones, and the like.

"Can I come there sometime?" she asked.

The plane leveled off and we'd been flying a while when I noticed that a blanket of clouds had obscured the ground and I hadn't felt my usual fear of takeoff. Jen wanted a headset to plug in the movie and listen to music in the meantime. I leaned back to close my eyes for a few moments.

At last, the timing was perfect. But Jen was only thirteen, and knowing how vulnerable teenagers are, I felt a pang of worry about leaving her alone every day. I couldn't forget the scare from that doorman who used to work in our building. Divorce had clearly inflicted a heavy burden on Jen. I watched helplessly as she struggled daily to adjust to life without her father. With my voice dismissed as a "scorned woman's" prejudice, there wasn't anyone to speak for Jenny. How different things might have been if that stepparent therapist had chosen to advocate on behalf of the child. The muffled sounds of a rock beat from Jen's headset broke through my thoughts. I squeezed her hand and wondered if she felt as helpless as I did.

I returned her smile as her body moved slightly to the beat. How sweet, innocent, and beautiful she looked. I wondered if the cultural inequities for women like me, who choose to be home for their children, would impact her life. Love and concern filled my heart.

Everything had changed for the baby John and I had tried six months to conceive. Jen wouldn't benefit anymore from the plans we had made to provide a good, stable home life for our kids, or from the joy recorded by her parents in photographs that fill our home. John and I had been pretty good at taking pictures, often delighting when we got the prints from the lab. Our plan was to make a gallery of family pictures in our dream home one day. John had left our box of pictures behind and they wouldn't ever hang in his gallery now. His plans had changed. I thought of other women, out there alone, scrambling to make a life and a family for their children after their husband's plans had changed. *If you want to make God laugh, tell Him your plans.* I took a deep breath and tried to think about happier things, like Johnny and the others waiting to see us.

Sunbleached and handsome, a young man could be seen in the crowd. Pale blue eyes, made more prominent by the California tan, sparkled like sunbeams kissing the ocean. When Jenny squealed, "There's Johnny!" his wide grin lit up the airport.

Molly was delighted to hear that I was gainfully employed. She had said I'd find a job soon, but I still worried that Jen might need me now more than ever. Molly reassured me that I'd be there when Jen did need me, saying, "You'll make the time." Molly pointed out that I had helped John and now he should be there to help me.

My sister Joan said I worried too much. It would be fun to work in advertising, and Jen would be fine. She asked, "When we were little no one was home and we turned out okay, didn't we?"

Dodi had returned to the States after traveling around Europe shooting films with her husband. She reminded me of that conversation we'd had years ago about her ex-husband and how she hadn't been willing to cope with his passive nature. She insisted that if I hadn't pushed John, he probably wouldn't have a career at all. Dodi agreed to stand by her words, offering to testify in court if John started withholding money. "You've earned at least a manager's percentage," she said.

Everyone agreed that it was important for me to have an interesting job, but we had built John's career together, and no matter what, I must fight for my share of his earnings. People who loved me had my best interests at heart, but we all knew that most of my share would go to the next wife. Though we talked about money, and I felt grateful for the emotional support, what was tearing me apart everyday was losing the family I had dreamed of for so long. No amount of money could recover that.

I wanted to get over my resentment toward John, but being in California was like returning to the scene of the crime. Each friend surfaced with examples of how I hadn't been fair to myself. I was urged to take off my rose-colored glasses and face a few unpleasant facts. But I couldn't make any changes as long as I was in California. I decided to forget about the past, enjoy my visit, and remind John when we returned that an increase in the support payment was long overdue.

All too soon our stay was at an end and we were flying east toward home. The usual worry returned. Would migraine headaches interfere with my work? Would Jennifer be safe in the city? How in the world would I get everything done when there's so much to do everyday? What I really needed was a wife! As the plane prepared for landing, I insisted to Jennifer that she must never hesitate to phone me at work.

My sister Joan was right, advertising was fun and since I'd once worked as an actor in commercials, it was especially interesting to watch the process from the beginning. Before long, Jen came to check things out.

"It took ten flights of stairs to get here on the subway," she said as her body and school books dropped into a chair. "By the time I go home, it'll be twenty."

She reminded me of what made me laugh every day. "After just five or six, I'm huffing and puffing like an old lady and pulling myself up by the rail. But pretty soon I'll be in great shape! A definite perk."

One after another my coworkers came by to meet my daughter and many were impressed by her beauty and gentle good manners. I, as always, was proud.

It was wonderful to watch my typing speed improve, although migraine headaches turned out to be a formidable challenge. My boss was sensitive. When my eyes would cloud over from ordinary daylight, made intolerable by the headache, she would open an empty, darkened office and allow me to rest for an hour. I really did like the job, but it required longer hours than I had expected, and it was tough trying to keep tabs on Jennifer. With too little time for myself, my fastidious ways changed. For a few months, housekeeping was virtually neglected.

It was 1983, and Jen had turned fourteen. She began testing the waters. I had succeeded in building trust with my daughter, but when I set rules of behavior, she said my level of trust in her was lacking. The "no-makeup-until-sixteen" rule could not be enforced because all the other girls were wearing lipstick and eye shadow! But it wasn't easy to keep quiet when Jennifer decided to copy Cleopatra.

Life in a fragmented family has enough problems so I tried to

203

be tolerant in areas that had less potential for long-term harm such as makeup. I took stock of the issues and decided to scale down wherever possible. The Rudolf Steiner School required that every student play an instrument. Jen had decided to learn to play the flute. Arguments about practicing added to the stress of homework, so I promised to drop the lessons if she agreed to devote more time to study. Her music teacher was disappointed.

"Jennifer has a natural lip for the instrument and an unusual talent."

Jen made a fish with her lips in the mirror and said, "But I hate to practice." I kept my promise.

The situation in school seemed to get worse as Jen's ninth year wore on. There were squabbles with friends, problems with teachers, and Jen's taste in clothes changed to a preference for basic black. A new teacher had been hired that year. He started a drama club and Jennifer was one of the first to join. It turned out to be a godsend. Studying drama was the only thing that made going to school bearable, even though the teacher demanded that schoolwork had to come first. Jennifer loved performing in plays, so the ultimate challenge was keeping teachers happy while doing as little homework as possible. I was caught in the middle.

Winter arrived and Manhattan turned into a glorious wonderland of bare branches, dripping icicles of frozen rain, and a fresh blanket of snow to cover the dirt. My work was becoming second nature and Jen was plotting her destiny.

One day Jen asked, "Mommy, do you think Daddy would let me visit the set of his new show?" When *Love of Life* was dropped by the network, John was cast on another daytime drama, *Search for Tomorrow*. I didn't know any of the cast or crew, but I was sure it would be fine.

204

"Of course, let's ask." I hoped he wouldn't say no. This time Dad agreed to the idea and a date was set for a visit. I wanted Jen to do some bonding with her father and she was excited about seeing real actors work. Her eyes were dancing with excitement when I kissed her good-bye. But I didn't expect what actually happened.

That night I was barely able to decipher the flood of words as she told the whole story. It had been fun meeting the cast and everyone was so nice. When Dad took her to lunch in the commissary, there were actors having their lunch who looked just like they do on television. The best news was saved for last.

"Mommy, they're looking for a young actress to play the part of a girl my age and I got up the nerve to ask if I could have an audition and you won't believe what they said. They're going to let me test for the part! Can I? Daddy's agent will handle the deal, and I'm getting really nervous. I probably can't memorize all those lines. I'll work extra hard on my homework. Can I do it, Mommy?"

In that split second, all the things I had heard about children working in the business flashed through my mind. They were legend. On the other hand, there were exceptions. This might be exactly what Jenny needed to prepare for the career she was determined to have. In that moment Jen won the argument I'd had with myself.

The character she would play was a runaway girl who is disguised as a boy. Jen had cut her long hair short by then and would be perfect for the part. The studio sent several pages of dialogue for the screen test and I filled in as the father to help her memorize the scene. The big day arrived. Early that morning a nervous young lady went off to the studio to have her first screen test and returned home with a seasoned actor's worry.

"Mommy, they said I was good but I know I could do better if they'd let me do it again."

It sounded familiar. I said she must try not to worry, because every actor has the same feelings after every audition. Her father said she did fine, but Jen was introduced to the agony of an actor waiting to hear who got the job.

For days she would phone me at work to ask if anyone had called, and then, as if I didn't know, she'd add, "No one's called here either. Do you think I should call Dad?" John was patient with the phone calls and when another actress was auditioned for the part, he told her gently that no decision had been made.

"You must be patient a little longer," I urged. It was asking a lot of a fourteen-year-old, but, all things considered, she handled it well.

Then word came that they decided to hire the other girl because she had years of experience and Jenny had virtually none. The young actress, however, was waiting to hear about a pending movie deal so she couldn't, as yet, accept the part on *Search*. With no definitive answer from the other girl, Jen continued to hope. She reasoned that the waiting would soon be over and besides, that's show business. I knew she was well-suited for an acting career.

One evening, with patience nearly gone, Jen dashed for the ringing telephone and, thank God, it was the studio. The message was complicated. The episode that was to introduce the runaway girl was scheduled to be taped the next day, but the other actress still couldn't give a final answer. They wanted Jen to do them a favor. Since the character was wearing a disguise and no one would actually be able to identify the person, they wanted Jennifer to work the opening show. If the other girl got the movie role, then Jennifer would be cast as the runaway. This decision was fraught with potential for great disappointment but she said, "Mommy, I want to work with Dad." It was fine with me, I cautioned, provided she really understood that she might only work one day. Jen said she understood, but I feared that deep down inside she didn't believe it.

Jen went to the studio for her first professional job as an actress and that evening came home and fell apart. When I put the disjointed pieces together, I knew why. The morning had gone as usual, with the first full-cast reading, followed by a rehearsal to block the moves, and then all the actors went to wardrobe and makeup.

Jenny had a hard time talking. "Mommy, we were just about ready to tape the show when the producer called me into her office. I was sure she was going to tell me I had the part and it was time to sign the contracts."

Jen was talking and sobbing at the same time.

"She told me that the other girl didn't get the movie and would be at the studio in time for the taping. She thought I'd be happy to know they were going to give me a whole day's pay even though I could go home then."

My heart was breaking as she went on.

"I didn't care about the money, I just wanted to do one taping with Dad."

She was really crying now. This youngster was learning the business. I held her in my arms and wished I'd been there when it happened.

My big bed had always been the place to recover so I tucked her in and pressed the blankets securely around her. I sat on the edge and tried to brush the disappointment from her brow and with utmost conviction told her a secret. I said even though she

207

was really feeling terrible now, she must try to be brave because everyone has to bear a certain amount of pain in life. I was sure her pain was coming early because she was going to be successful at a very young age. She would get wonderful parts as an actress and not have to endure the years of rejection most actors suffer without ever making it. She was silently listening to every word. "I think you're going to be luckier than most and maybe God wants you to understand how the others feel so He's given you this experience before you're too busy and famous to notice."

Before very long she smiled, "I'm okay now, Mommy. What's for dinner?"

It had been a brutal introduction to a brutal business, but the amazing thing was that it didn't discourage Jen in the least. She wanted to be an actress now more than ever, and I lost the homework war.

Jen was becoming a well-defined, independent person. If I tried to hold her back, she would become more inventive, and at times you could almost feel the tension between us. But our strong bond of trust remained intact and the lines of communication stayed open. She came to me with a steady stream of growing-girl problems as she reflected her independence in her taste in clothes and by continuing to cut her beautiful hair that everyone admired. The real problem areas were curfew, where she was allowed to go and with whom, and the never-ending homework war.

The drama club was planning to end the year with a play and everyone was invited. Jen was excited to hear that her classmates thought she'd be wonderful as the leading lady. At dinner I learned how much she wanted that part, so I began to help every day with homework. Just before the audition she said, "I hope Daddy comes this time."

208

Well, some of her homework was still missing, so Jen didn't get the lead. She learned that rules are rules and are not to be broken, but she did get to play the second lead.

I watched her place "reserved" signs on some seats up front to make sure Daddy could see the stage. He had promised to come but I couldn't relax until, at last, I saw him walk in. When Jen took her bow, the room filled with applause. She really was good and I was more proud than ever. She ran off to celebrate with her Dad and his party in a very elegant restaurant. He really came through.

Before the school year ended, Jen said we needed to talk. "Mom, my friend told me that there's a school near us that's just like the one in the movie *Fame* and they teach classes in acting for kids who want to be actors. A girl told my friend what it's like and, Mommy, I really want to go there. Anyway, I want to find a different school because last year was really terrible. I know I'll do better where other kids are more like me."

She made a good case. "It sounds like you've thought it through carefully, so if you're absolutely sure, find out what we need to do to enroll and I'll help you from there."

Jennifer set right to work making phone calls. I was impressed with how well she gathered the information. But the outcome wasn't good.

"Mommy, I've missed the auditions!" She was stopped in her tracks by the disappointing news that auditions for the next semester had already been held.

"No one can be admitted without auditioning to see if they have talent because thousands of kids apply every year."

"What about eleventh grade?"

"No! You have to enroll by tenth grade. I won't ever be able to go there!"

I was as disappointed for Jen as she was for herself. "Maybe I can think of something. We hire a lot of actors in advertising. Maybe someone at work can help."

Several people said they'd make a few phone calls to see if there just might be a chance that she was given the wrong information. I even got John to ask his friends at the studio if they knew anyone who was in a position to help. The weeks dragged on and the summer was hot. One by one, our people were told there were absolutely no late auditions. We would just have to accept it. Even Jen said, "I guess we have to, Mom. Thanks anyway."

I refused to accept it. If there was a school that nurtures talent, then my gifted daughter should be going there. She had to get in.

I then thought of our old friends who lived in my building. Susan Dooley's husband, John, worked at a high-level job in education. Jen had once read a part in an original play that was performed at his school. He often commented that Jennifer had talent. I phoned Susan. "Do you think John would mind if I asked for a favor?"

With the same spirit of helpfulness that helped me decorate Jennifer's bedroom, she gave me John's number at work. When I called, he said there was a guy who just happened to owe him a favor. He'd call me back soon.

A few days later, John's deep, cultured voice said, "Jennifer has an audition the day after tomorrow. Have her prepare a scene that runs a minute and a half and, this is important, she absolutely must show up because it's her last chance. They're holding only one late audition."

"Don't worry, she'll be there!"

"Mom, I'm so happy. Wait, I don't have a scene." So I took a Neil Simon play to work the next day and found a scene between a father and his daughter, edited out the father, and trimmed it to a minute and a half. She went over the lines, again and again, until it was time for the audition. When it was over she was a bundle of nerves. "But Mom, what if after all that I don't get in?"

We waited all summer, but the call didn't come. It was the last weekend before the new semester started and things didn't look good. Jen went to her dad's for the weekend, fighting disappointment, and planning to go back to the Rudolf Steiner School on Monday morning.

Early Monday morning I was jarred awake by the ringing telephone and a woman's voice asked for Jennifer. I said she wasn't home but that I was her mother and the woman said, "Tell her if she can be here by eight o'clock sharp, we'll admit her to the High School of Performing Arts today." The details are a bit fuzzy, but I can remember my excitement clearly. Jen got there before eight and it was the best break she ever had.

Our friends the Dooleys had made a big contribution to Jen's future. Thanks to John, my daughter would have the benefit of early preparation for her career in acting. I had the benefits of a much-needed job.

Chapter 15
A GIFT WITH EVERY PAIN

DESTINY HAD LAID A GENTLE hand of kindness on Jen and me. It was 1984 and women were still fighting for equality. I continued to find my job interesting and Jen seemed to fit right in at her new school. We both appreciated that she had been given a chance that remains only a fantasy in most young people's dreams. One night at dinner, Jen beamed, "Mom, it's just like the movie! Today at lunch everyone was singing and some kids were dancing on tables. I love my school."

My uneasiness relaxed with that news. The teachers, parents, kids, and the values taught at the Rudolf Steiner School had been familiar to me. This new school was still an unknown factor, and although I was sure that a solid foundation had been laid, most of my parenting time was spent at work. I wanted Jen to at least be happy and it was comforting to hear that she was.

Taking the last bite off my plate, I noticed a frown on Jenny's face. "What's wrong?" I wondered out loud.

"On the way home from school I was waiting at a crosswalk with a little old man and when the light changed I hurried across. But as I got to the other side, horns started honking real loud. I turned around and that poor old man was in the middle of the street with the light ready to change. He was trying to hurry but could barely walk. Mom he looked so scared. I went back to help, but those idiots kept right on honking!"

Jen had encountered an unpleasant fact that often surfaces under the pressure of city life.

"Honey, nice people can be unkind when they're driving in traffic and become blinded by the need to get going. They probably didn't even notice the man was old. It was good that you took time to offer help."

"Mom, whenever I see really old people it makes me want to cry, because everything they try to do is so hard."

"Darling, I know what you mean. I also have a soft spot for the elderly and even enjoy listening when Yaya repeats the same stories about life in Greece when she was young. I can see that she's reliving a time full of dreams and hope for the future. In those few moments she forgets the aches and pains of old age and that death could come any day."

"I can't stand to think about Yaya dying."

"We'll all be terribly sad." I realized that we hadn't seen her for a while. "Let's visit her next weekend."

Jen said, "It's nice to sit here and talk after dinner."

"I like it, too."

"At Dad's I don't get to."

"Don't get to what?"

214

"Right after I finish eating I have to leave the table."

"Why do you have to do that?"

"Because it's grown-up time to talk without being interrupted by childish comments."

That was a surprise to hear, since I found her fascinating. "They don't know what they're missing. I love talking with you."

"No biggie," she said and started clearing the table.

Considering how much Jen adored her father, it was impressive to watch this issue roll off her back. A mother feels pain when her children get hurt and I wondered if at this point I felt more pain than Jen. I was learning that raising children is a big responsibility to carry alone. Society's impulse to have two-parent families had come from practical experience. As one doing it alone, I always worried that I might be either giving too much support or yelling too much about homework. I sure hoped the new school would stimulate in Jen more incentive for study. But was I doing my job as a parent?

Though I was classified as part-time at work, it wasn't reflected in the long hours I put in or very evident in my salary. I had been at the agency for more than a year and heard about more interesting jobs that paid better wages. Since everyone was happy with my work, I hoped they might give me a chance to move up the ladder. With that in mind, I mustered the courage to make an appointment with the vice president.

Entering his large, lavish office, I was surprised to find my knees shaking on the long walk across the pale green carpet to his desk. When our short talk ended, I stood up to leave and nearly knocked myself out on the glass ceiling.

Apparently it was more difficult to find a high-quality woman to do my job than to find someone to fill a higher position.

215

Finding a good support staff for the office was a never-ending problem. It appeared that women were being liberated from taking care of their husbands at home and were reluctant to take care of someone else's in the office. The venue had changed but from what I'd seen in our office, for most women, the expectations were pretty much the same.

One observation was validated: they did like my work because my status changed from part-time to full with all the benefits, and even a raise was part of the package as long as I didn't mention promotion again.

I accepted the full-time position and made the most of it. Jen was happy in school. She was getting up early without any prompting in order to be one of the first to arrive. "Mom, I can't wait to get there because we're improvising scenes and doing unbelievable acting exercises, too."

Life was settling into a peaceful routine.

I was minding my own sweet receptionist's business when menopause hit with a vengeance. I sat looking lovely, surrounded by mirrors that reflected a bright red flush on my face. I sweltered from the furnace that burned in my breast. Waves of heat parched my mouth and beads of sweat covered my brow as the telephones rang, people arrived, packages were sent and delivered, and secretaries said to do this and that. In the middle of my passage through middle age, there was an unexpected call from Jen's school. Homework had been missing for sometime and she'd been absent seventeen days. I snapped into the phone, "Why have you waited so long to call?"

"Your child's homework and attendance are not our responsibility, dear."

Jen and I started having terrible arguments, but no matter

how much I threatened, yelled, or punished she hated doing homework and liked taking days off from school. There was too much unsupervised time on her hands. What she needed was a job. The idea was a winner but she couldn't find a job near our house. I came up with an even better plan.

In my office, a part-time person covered in reception for two hours at the end of the day. It would be perfect if Jen were hired to fill that position. My boss liked the idea, too. Jen would learn about advertising and earn pretty decent money for a first job. So my daughter began working in my office for two hours everyday after school. She caught on quickly as I knew she would and with so much in common to share, I felt we were becoming more like friends.

Jen was becoming even more independent.

Tired of my nagging, she had toned down the Cleopatra makeup but continued to wear black. Her somewhat radical hair-style brought a variety of comments. The left side was chopped above the ear and the right was crimped to hang over one eye and down to the chin. On anyone else it might have looked odd, but on Jen it was extremely attractive and everyone thought so, too. Yaya was puzzled. "How can she see? Why does she dress like a widow?"

New school jackets were chosen that year and Jen was happy when they selected black satin. The Performing Arts logo with comedy and tragedy masks was embroidered in red on the back and the student's name stitched in small red script above the left breast. There were many new friends who came to our house and when the jackets arrived, they all wore them together and felt pride in their school.

One day after work I was simply too tired to face the crush of people on a subway, so I decided to take the bus home. Standing in front of me, facing the other direction, was a shiny black jacket with that familiar red logo. I tapped the satin shoulder and a beautiful young girl turned around.

"Do you go to Performing Arts High School?" I asked.

"Yes, I do. Why?"

"Because my daughter, Jennifer Aniston, does, too, and I thought you might know her."

"Oh, JoJen," she squealed, "We all call her JoJen because there are so many Jennifers in school. I love her! Everybody loves her. Oh my God, you're her Mom. I'm so glad to meet you. I just love her!"

The bus bounced toward home and we talked about how lucky the kids were to study acting and music and dance in high school. Soon it was time for me to get off. I walked home from my stop wrapped in the warmth of spring, happy just to be alive. With both parents and my husband gone, I was no longer a daughter or a wife, but I was definitely somebody's mother!

I arrived home to find icing on the cake. I found a message on the answering machine announcing that Penelope Savalas had moved to Manhattan and was living right near our house. A perfect ending to the day.

That Jennifer's godsister was living in the city brought many blessings to our life. At last we had family nearby, which made everything, especially holiday dinners, more special.

There were visits from Jen's godparents, too. Penelope gave a party for her mother and it was fascinating to be with Lynn in that totally different environment. We talked about the changes we'd both experienced since the days in California when our kids were young. We recalled how everything had turned out so differently than we'd planned. Most of the guests were Penelope's friends, but they managed to make two moms feel like part of the gang.

John married his girlfriend and shortly thereafter they moved

218

to Los Angeles. What an odd state of affairs: I continued to live in the city where we had moved to pursue his career and he moved to the place I called home. Molly said it was more of an irony. Jennifer wondered how her father could move so far away and I remembered, a long time ago, wondering the same thing about my own mother.

"Mom, today I learned that some kids have pictures taken of themselves, by professional photographers, called headshots. I need some, too."

I understood the importance of what she was asking. Good headshots are the key to an agent's success in booking auditions. The agent submits an actor's picture for a part and from that picture the casting director decides whether or not to request an audition. The decision is made primarily on the looks of the actor. I made an appointment for a sitting with a photographer. Not one shot turned out well. They had cost a fortune and there wasn't a single picture we liked! I remembered that years ago John and I took great headshots of each other. Maybe I still had the knack.

I borrowed a 35mm camera and taught Jen the correct way to apply makeup. The result surprised even me. The pictures were so good that her friends wanted to know if I would take their headshots, too. It delighted me no end when they liked their pictures as well. I bought a good camera with a portrait lens and started to study photography. The kids from Jen's school gave me lots of opportunities to practice and I played with the idea of starting a little business on the side.

As Jen grew toward womanhood and life became more complicated, we had long talks to interpret its mysteries.

I'd been dating a couple of interesting men but was still pretty guarded and unwilling to get too close. I really didn't like being without a man, so when I found myself more and more attracted to a tall, charming producer, I decided to give it a chance.

He commuted from another town and it was difficult to find time for each other, which was fine with me because I didn't have much time to date. This was a perfect situation. It was increasingly evident that we really were good together and I knew I cared more than I should. Jen liked him, too, and saw how wonderfully compatible we were. One day she asked, "Why don't you two get married?"

The truth became abundantly clear after our next date. I came home hiding my tears. You see, he was married. How perfect.

Jen said again, "Mom, don't you think he'd make a wonderful husband?"

Tears moistened my eyes. "Darling, he already is."

"Well, if he's seeing you, she can't make him very happy!"

My daughter had expressed a view right out of the common rhetoric. I had heard it many times before and had even thought it myself. However, at this point in time, my views had radically changed.

"Honey, that reasoning has fed men who behave badly for years and if a man can't keep his vows, you shouldn't blame his wife. A person's morality is not the responsibility of anyone but himself. I couldn't live with the knowledge that another woman was going through the hell of a broken family because of me. No, Sweetie, it won't be easy but I'm not going to see him again."

From the look on Jen's face, I could see that she understood the full meaning of what I'd said. I hoped that a seed had been planted that would blossom as a real moral value in the future.

Because I cared for him deeply it took months to get over that man. Each night I'd curl up in the fetal position, cry from missing his essence, and fall asleep only after I'd promised myself to call him tomorrow. But in the light of day I'd think of that woman facing holidays alone or standing next to me at her child's graduation. I never saw him again. Statistics show that more than sixty percent of the males who initiate divorce leave for another woman. Maybe if more women refused to be part of that equation, fewer families would suffer.

The office was buzzing with rumors of a corporate buyout and soon the talk became fact. Around 1986, our company merged with a bigger agency and moved to another location. There was no longer a permanent position for Jen. My job and the whole atmosphere in the agency changed considerably. My naturally helpful nature made others suspicious and I got a real education in how women treat women at work.

I'd been setting my alarm for five in the morning to do household chores such as laundry before leaving to open the office at eight. This left my evenings free to help Jen with school assignments. The long days had me exhausted and I was no longer happy at work. The new employees that came with the merger brought an element of competition that was devoid of appreciation and kindness. People I'd been happy working with gradually changed. Others were fired. I wanted desperately to resign, but I couldn't put myself through the agony of looking for another job, so I dragged myself to work, wishing I were somewhere else.

I made some calculations and found that there was still a deficit in my support payments from John. For sometime he had failed to send an amount that would have included all of the yearly increase called for in our divorce agreement. John was living in California and via long distance I had been appealing to him for months. He gave a variety of reasons why he couldn't send more, and in a most unpleasant tone, accused me of being greedy. Nothing in our seventeen years together ever indicated that! When I could no longer take the insults, I would let it pass. Now with my job uncertain and the future looking scary, I knew it was time to make him comply. John's excuses would no longer hold water.

Talking on the telephone became too unpleasant so I started writing letters. A particularly scathing response from Los Angeles was the final straw, so I hired a lawyer. By then John was very popular on the daytime series *Days of Our Lives* and as the attractive villain Victor Kiriakis, he was being considered for two Emmys. He was enjoying the fruits of our joint efforts. I couldn't imagine how he could be stingy with me of all people. I finally got angry. My lawyer read his letters and advised me not to take the disrespect. He said he'd work it out on my behalf. He did.

John finally complied with the financial terms of our divorce agreement. And not a moment too soon because not long after that I lost my job.

An unfortunate encounter with a taxi cab severely damaged my knees. A therapist prescribed that I rest my legs for extended periods each day, saying that if I wanted to avoid arthritis in my later years, I mustn't return to work. They had no choice but to let me go.

The review of my past continued to make new impressions on my thinking. Recalling that after losing my job everything had turned out well gave me a new confidence. With still no communication between Jen and me, I could better accept that our separation would, in the end, bring gains. It was clear that rebuilding my life after divorce had made me stronger and more independent than I otherwise would have been. I was beginning to see that life is a never-ending adventure that gives us a gift with every pain.

A mountain shifted within and I knew I would be with Jen again when this most recent lesson was learned.

Chapter 16
SEEDS FOR A NEW LIFE

A S SPRING SIZZLED INTO SUMMER I was becoming stronger and more confident every day. Memories revealed that a lot of water had passed under my life's bridge since growing up, getting married, divorced, and starting over were part of everyday life. Eventually, good had always come with the changing conditions of my life. If hard times in the past had brought gains, then so would this terrible separation from Jen. Some ground had already been cleared and, once again, I was planting seeds for a new life in the rocky soil of pain. I was on the path from self-pity to acceptance. I opened the windows, aired out the house, and quit smoking.

But there were also the proverbial steps back and the daily challenge to stay centered. A random thought or some insignificant incident could rekindle the pain to full force. A friend of mine named Coral Leigh, before retiring in the early nineties, had worked as a manager for young actors. One day Coral came to me with startling news. She had learned that tabloid TV had been so unfair to actors that many were boycotting the shows, and that the tabloid show I had been on was the worst offender. I wanted to fade into thin air. How stupid I felt. Was this why Jen was so angry?

I talked it over with my friend Bari. She always lent support, but also had a gentle way of telling me the truth. "Don't be too hard on yourself. Jen might justifiably be annoyed, but an estrangement is overreacting. I still believe it's her cry for independence."

The media blitz surrounding the popularity of *Friends* continued to print misleading quotes about my past and I still harbored a terrible doubt that Jen had actually told them those things. One particularly heartless article reported that as a teenager Jen had tried to run away from home. She was to meet a friend who had agreed to help her, but the friend didn't show up so Jen was forced to return home. Where was I? Did she pack a suitcase? What was so terrible at home? It tore me apart to read that Jen had been that unhappy yet didn't tell me. We'd always spoken freely about everything. Doesn't the press realize how hurtful it is for a mother to read such a thing in a magazine? Do the parents of other celebrities feel the same? For weeks I was haunted by the image of Jen packing and leaving our home. I wanted to share this with Johnny but I knew it would place him right in the middle. I continued to wait for him to call me.

It was getting hotter as the approaching date of my late July birthday ushered in another wave of depression. Still no word from Jen or Johnny. The due date of my first grandchild was near.

224

The possibility that this terrible loss would also include my son and his family threatened to burst the hope I retained.

It had been a great source of joy to know that I had never spent a birthday without at least one of my children. As the day drew near, their absence became unbearable. I was missing them more than ever. Despite telling myself it was going to be all right, I tried to prepare for the worst. It helped that my calendar was filled with lunch dates to celebrate with friends, and lovely greeting cards eased my depression. But the absence of my kids had me secretly dreading that day.

Then I received a most wonderful telephone call. Penelope Savalas was flying into Los Angeles and wanted to have dinner with me. There was some business matter to settle, time was short, and she had only one night that was free. God does work miracles. That one night just happened to be on my birthday and I just happened to be free.

We made plans to dine at a neighborhood restaurant and I started looking forward to my special day. Penelope didn't know that the date of our dinner fell on my birthday and I decided not to tell her. Penelope herself could brighten anybody's day. I was going to be with someone I loved very much and just being together was special enough.

We both ordered salads to maintain our slim bodies and chatted like kids after school. The food was good and the conversation great. What a lovely birthday this turned out to be. Warmed by that thought, I couldn't resist sharing that it was my birthday. Her big brown eyes sparkled as she expressed her delight in her own sweet Penelope way. When she asked where the kids were, my newfound strength simply vanished and I started to cry. It was embarrassing to fall apart like that but she made it seem all

225

right. I didn't want to tell her what happened but the truth slowly eked out. She expressed regret for all of us. She loved her god-sister and Johnny and I knew how she felt about me. She never took sides, but the things that she said helped in so many ways. She spoke quietly of an incident that happened many years ago.

As often happens with young girls, there had been a misunderstanding with her mother that sent her hailing a taxi to Papa. She railed on and on as Telly patiently let her vent all the anger. Then she waited to receive his support. Instead, he got stern and said he'd kick her fanny if she ever spoke that way about her mother again. He'd given his support to Lynn! My tears began to flow once again. Telly could have been the hero and made points with his daughter, but he knew that the best he could give, for the rest of her life, was to protect the bond with her mother. Penelope said his reaction shocked her into a view she had not seen before.

I wanted to phone Telly to express my admiration for the high quality of his character that had instilled the same in his daughter. But a couple of years earlier a wicked cancer proved stronger than his bountiful spirit and we found ourselves gathered for his funeral in the same church where, many years earlier, baby Jennifer was christened. As we spoke, I saw a familiar twinkle in Penelope's eyes and somehow I knew Telly had heard my praise.

We talked a long time and it was surprising to observe that someone so young had one-half of her understanding in Jen's world and the other half in mine. She explained that as grown women, she and her sister, Candace, often had entirely different interpretations of the same events in their childhood. I told Penelope it looked like many of my recollections are different than Jen's and that I hoped one day we could reconcile the differences.

226

She reminded me of how close Jenny and I had been before Jenny left home. Penelope believed that one day Jen and I would be close again. She was happy to hear that I had both good friends and church to give me support in the meantime.

It was time to think of happier things. Penelope had moved out of New York City and there was a lot of catching up to do. We went back to my house and talked late into the night. It was fun reminiscing about the old days in California when my children were little and Lynn brought Penelope and Candace, to play in our half-finished house.

We chuckled as she recalled how it had been a great honor when Johnny invited a girl up to play in his tree house, but that poor Jen was too little to climb and had to stay down below. Penelope also recalled that when they were playing a game in Johnny's room, he made Jenny say a password before she could enter and the secret word was the name of a Dallas Cowboy football player. She had been impressed that little three-year-old Jennifer never failed to remember the name. We laughed as I learned, so many years later, what had gone on while Lynn and I were busy talking.

After Penelope left, I laid in bed, sleepless for a few moments, thinking about Jen. What part had she played? In counseling sessions Reverend Jim said that even if Jen hadn't been a perfect daughter, I mustn't ever want her to change because the only person we have a right to change is ourselves. During the year of counseling sessions following my divorce in the early eighties, my very wise therapist, Barbara Callen, told me the same thing about John as she urged me to look within myself for answers. I wanted so much to call Jen but at last I, too, believed we needed more time.

It had been a wonderful birthday and I thanked God for

another miracle. I fell asleep with visions of our innocent young children bringing a smile to my face.

Soon everything changed for the better. A letter in my daughter-in-law's handwriting arrived. My heart raced as I stared at the envelope. Inside was an ultrasound picture of my unborn grandchild glued to a handwritten note that sent the imaginary words of greeting, "I love you, Grandmother." I gazed at technology's image of the miracle of birth and said to that hint of our baby, "Maybe I won't lose you, too." A deep respect for Shannon had already been growing and now her special qualities became even more apparent. This considerate gesture had demonstrated the full extent of her sensitivity and a wisdom beyond her years. I was happy to know that my son had found this lovely young woman to share his life.

It was time to telephone my daughter-in-law. I dialed with love and respect in my heart. We met for lunch and I felt the baby kick as we both glowed with anticipation. She said Johnny was excited about it, too. A month later the baby was born and my son, himself, telephoned with the news! Tears flowed as I raced to the maternity ward. Holding his tiny daughter for the first time awakened feelings of love from a depth I hadn't felt since the birth of my own babies. Being a grandmother was better than I'd ever been told and it was wonderful to experience that human beings have such an enormous capacity for love.

Johnny didn't say a word about his sister. I had interpreted his absence as a gesture to remain neutral and would now extend the same to his silence. If anything needed to be said, in time, he would let me know.

When my granddaughter was four months old, Shannon returned to her job as a store manager. Because Johnny worked part-time as a freelance assistant director, he became Mr. Mom and I volunteered to be the fill-in baby-care Grandmom. A most wonderful, joyous bond developed as a little baby girl completely captured my heart. It was a peculiar dichotomy: one part of me couldn't mention Jen's name without crying and the other was overflowing with joy. Months of caring for that precious baby did help rebuild a significant part of my life, though one important thing was missing from the joy. I loved being a grandmother and I wished I could share it with Jen.

I told myself one day the time will be right to greet our family's newest member together and what a wonderful day that will be. Hope was the force inching me forward.

My friends said they were glad I quit smoking and that it was sure about time I got happy.

Shifts in my thinking continued to take place. Free from the prison of fear, I now had the courage to examine unresolved feelings about my past history with John. Despite all I had done to help him, he had left me for another woman, which had further damaged my already lagging self-worth. Through the years my interest in taking a chance with another mate had waned. I sometimes wondered if it might be easier if John would just say, "Thank you" or "I'm sorry." I wanted to weed out that last vestige of dependence.

I decided to edit the section in my journal where I'd recorded my marriage, divorce, and the difficult years that followed. With a box of tissues nearby, I spent days reliving every detail and feeling. The realization was slow in coming, but come it did— John really didn't need to apologize.

A liberating truth moved in like the tide, pervading the cracks in my thinking; from behind the curtain of inequity it appeared that John had actually been my perfect mate. I could see that a childhood of rejection had conditioned me to be the sacrificing victim, making few demands for myself, yet willing to do anything to help John advance his career. Each time I pushed him toward his goal or convinced him to take a step that improved our situation, I became more confident that he would never leave me. Though he didn't mention it, I felt sure that my husband was grateful, even dependent on me. Conversely, he probably interpreted my help as nagging and his giving in to my "demands" as helping me. Hence, John's comment during our divorce negotiations, "I've done all I'm going to do for you." Sounded like the men-and-women-are-from-different-planets theory. Two people were caught in a dynamic that needed serious counseling to fix and neither understood where the other was coming from. There were shadings of a modern version of O. Henry's short story "Gift of the Magi": each gave what the other wanted, only in our version there was no happy ending. Neither of us felt thankful to the other. A lot of resentment can build up that way. It was hard to face as years of believing I had been a good wife vanished under my own harsh scrutiny. It was abundantly clear, at last, why human beings must leave each other free.

John and I both had weaknesses to overcome and when he had incentive to end our marriage, as usually happens in divorce, human frailty tends to surface. I suspected that our flaws had joined in classic symbiosis to give us both a chance to learn what being together had failed to teach us: independence, fairness, and forgiveness.

For the first time in many years warm feelings for John returned and brought the final closure I was seeking. I no longer felt taken advantage of. I had learned that helping someone

230

should never guarantee even gratitude in return. Help given or received in the right way must stand on its own.

I still believe that for Jenny's sake and mine, John's departure might have been more gradual and that considering the hard times we'd been through together, I deserved better treatment after our divorce. However, it's no secret that anger, justified or not, is a stimulus for action. A lifetime of events was showing me that when other people make choices that adversely affect me or even change the rules in the middle of the game, I needn't carry the guilt and shame.

Finding my role in contributing to the outcome was liberating. The fact that every human being has faults that add to the world's misery had me hoping that I had lessened it a bit by accepting responsibility for some of mine. It wasn't easy to admit to being so flawed, but as I accepted my own mistakes it became easier to accept other people's. I could even imagine that weeks of torment must have preceded John's abrupt decision to leave his family.

I can now accept that I'll never receive what I think is adequate compensation for my contribution to John's success. Like any two partners dissolving a business, I believe there should have been a more equitable financial arrangement. I understand that with John's acting career being our business, it's difficult to assess the level of compensation. However, my friend Robert, a divorce attorney, said there's case law precedent where the former wives of doctors and lawyers were awarded a percentage of their former spouses' future earnings. I believe this sign bodes well for women in the future. If the courts designate that a percentage be paid based on past contributing factors, the abandoned spouse will no longer be made to feel that she's taking money she didn't earn.

But I really can't blame John for our financial squabbles when millions of other men blatantly manipulate the courts to award even less. Consequently, most single mothers are forced to leave their children to be raised by others while they work outside the home. A rigorous accounting of child support money is demanded, which fosters the notion that child support belongs to the child—a view accepted by our legal system as well as our culture. No one thinks to ask if part of the household money would belong to the child if the marriage had remained intact. Along with the living expenses that impact a child's quality of life, compensation for the job of raising children is left out of the accounting. In this way the importance of motherhood is dramatically minimized. No wonder so few women want to do it full-time.

Partial blame lies in our widespread acceptance of the "Hell-hath-no-fury" theory, which further demeans women by reducing a woman's ability to rise above her feelings to less than a man's. A subsequent wife picks up the cliché and is home free to convince her husband that his ex-wife's concerns are not valid. With divorce on the rise, I hope to see the day when society demands that *all* parties involved cooperate with each other to raise the children.

In my view a social change, supported by our legal system, needs to take place. That kind of change always takes the concerted efforts of many, but I have vowed to spend what's left of my life as an advocate for mothers.

On a personal level, I knew that even if it meant living alone for the rest of my life I would never be anyone's victim again. With an abundance of warmth in my heart for the closure of another life-altering issue, I felt more than ready to continue my journey through time.

232

Chapter 17
LAUNCHING ANOTHER CAREER

MANY THINGS CHANGED IN THE two years following the end of my lackluster advertising "career." Firsthand knowledge had told me that twenty-five years as a mother doesn't exactly qualify one to climb the corporate ladder. Lacking college in a world obsessed with degrees convinced me that it would be best to start my own business. With my strength tending toward creativity I enrolled in some basic photography classes to increase my skills with a camera. The next step was to build a studio in Johnny's empty room.

For several weeks I visited stores in lower Manhattan that sold photographic equipment: lighting, back drops, props, reflectors, and the like. I would race for the subway at seven in the morning, hoping to arrive while the shop was still empty because the sales people, often out-of-work technicians, would let me pick their brains. In that rather awkward way I learned the business of photography and gradually, by trial and error, set up a pretty good studio. Jen's friends at school continued to need pictures and my talent with makeup was an unexpected bonus for them. Before long I needed an appointment book.

Jen sat patiently before my camera, allowing me to experiment with equipment or new methods of lighting. There was a perfect meeting of needs: she always had new pictures and I had a wonderful model. My work was turning out great, much better than I ever expected. When agents or managers saw one of my shots in an actresses portfolio, they would ask for the photographer's name and then send me their clients.

My business was growing, but it was not very profitable. Lab costs were high, and long hours pouring over proof sheets ate into profits. I knew how important it was for an actor to have the best shots possible. I felt confident that if I gave it all I had, one day financial gain would come.

I recalled the words of my therapist, Barbara Callen, who suggested that I would enjoy a profession that helped people with problems. Neither massage therapy nor counseling had been the right choice and I had invested a lot of time and money to prove the point. Had I, at last, found a career that would satisfy all of my needs?

In middle age, when hot flashes brought the return of rage, I became angry that my future was so unsure. It looked like I had made many poor choices. Wanting to spare Jen my hard lesson, when she was just fifteen, I began to encourage her to make herself financially secure before getting married and not to have children until then. I cautioned that stress over the lack of money can wear on the bonds that hold people together. I also spoke of my belief that children need to be cared for by a parent and it's not consistent with the children's needs if both parents work and leave them to be raised by others. I then urged her to arrange a future where she depended on only herself for security. I promised to help her achieve those aims. She listened to my suggestions and said, "Mom, don't worry. Things will be different with me. What I really need now is to learn how to drive."

People who remarked that I had courage to use my car in Manhattan now said I was plain nuts to teach Jennifer to drive there. But I had learned to drive where I lived and so would she. To learn the basics, we had the first two or three lessons in New Jersey when the malls were empty. My little Honda was built with a stick shift and I couldn't help laughing when we chugged around the parking lot, learning to release the clutch while slowly accelerating on the gas. When that maneuver became a smooth operation, the traffic, pot holes, and the rude, aggressive drivers of Manhattan became our practice field. I reasoned that if Jen could drive under these conditions, she could drive anywhere. When this harrowing experience was over and Jen received her license, I had developed more patience as well as courage, and I knew for sure that I was a little bit crazy.

Jenny was a senior by then and driving gave her even more independence. With so many friends and social activities, the time we spent together was becoming shorter and shorter. But there was still the need to consult with Mom as Jen began to encounter the constant and inevitable problems with friends. Unending squabbles and hurt feelings were puzzling because Jen was born with a natural ability to get along and preferred harmony. Although they were less frequent, we still had wonderful talks.

My business kept me busy but I missed Jen. I had to force

FROM MOTHER AND DAUGHTER TO FRIENDS

myself not to worry when she was tearing around the city in my car. (Please stay alert!) But she always touched base on the phone, and sometimes my business took so much time that I even forgot to worry. All in all, life was good and I rarely had to remind Jen about homework. I had become much too complacent.

In mid-year a call came from school. The girls' senior counselor alerted me to a reality I hadn't expected. A voice full of righteous indignation pointed the finger of blame right through the phone, saying, "Do you know your daughter may not graduate with her class?" Apparently when I let down on my policing, Jen let down on her homework. The woman said that so many assignments were missing that it wouldn't be possible to catch up and they probably wouldn't let her graduate.

Over my dead body, I thought, and I asked, "Is there anything I can do?"

"If the homework is brought up to date, and no more is missed until the end of the year, she might get passing marks on the finals and then maybe, just maybe, we'll let her pass." The senior counselor's voice exuded the power that comes when a person holds your destiny in her hands.

My role was clear: I would hit the books with Jen. Together we began a strict regimen of study. Despite the jam she was in, Jen took it all in stride. It was wonderful to discover that we both enjoyed learning about the variety of topics she brought to the table. We spent every evening studying things like English and literature that I'd long ago forgotten. I experienced the full scope of Jen's capable mind. More than once I tried to imagine my parents helping with homework. How things had changed.

Before long our focus split. The nightly study sessions continued but the major part of our concern shifted to the most important project of the school year. For Jen it was the most important project of her life.

There is a tradition at Performing Arts High that students don't perform before an audience until the senior play when the graduating class performs for the public. It's importance is legendary because many people from the entertainment business are invited and come to scout for new talent. The students hear of famous actors who had been discovered that way. Jen explained that senior plays could often lead to signing with an agent or even being cast in a part. During the performance talent agents jot down the names of kids they think have potential. It's part of the tradition for the principal to post a list of students' names with the name of the interested agent on the main bulletin board. For several days after the play closes, the hopeful actors race to see if their names are on the board.

I understood how important it was to have a good part and why Jen was so nervous. She worked harder than ever before on homework and was soon up to par with her class.

The teacher finally announced that he'd chosen the play but it took what seemed forever to start casting. From day to day the picture changed. One day it looked like Jenny might be cast in the lead and the next it looked like the part would go to someone else. The list of likely contenders kept growing. Jen tried to gain an edge by practicing all of the female parts, even if they had only a few lines, in order to prepare herself for the worst possible decision. "Mom, today I did so well in acting class that some kids I hardly knew said they were sure I was going to be cast as the princess. My grades are much better and if those kids are right, there's no reason I won't. I'm too excited to eat dinner." The next night she was just as sure that someone else would get the coveted part and was too depressed to eat.

"If they don't make up their minds pretty soon, you're going to be as thin as a rail."

"Am I really losing weight?" There had been some grumbling about weight.

It went on like this for what seemed an eternity and then the date for auditions was set. Jen tried not to set her heart on the lead and I mentioned that it really didn't matter, because she stood out on stage and would be noticed in any part. She said I was prejudiced and I agreed.

A visitor could actually feel the nervous tension in our house as wanting and trying not to want clashed on a minute to minute basis. There was nothing to do but wait.

At last the date for auditions was set. When it was over, Jen said the drama teacher had asked her to read for the second lead, too. She said the second lead would be just as good. As days passed, Jen nervously twisted her hair and came to the conclusion that even a smaller part would be okay.

The day she came home with the casting news was one of the hardest days of my life. They had chosen other girls for the lead, second lead, and all of the other speaking female parts. Jen would play a dancing girl who didn't have a single line to say.

Her voice sounded strange as she held back tears. "Mom, I thought if I had a good part Daddy would fly in from L.A."

"But darling he may still come if you ask."

"I don't want him to. Mom, I don't even have one word to say. I can't believe this has happened."

Trembling set in before she finished talking and I thought she was going to collapse. A strange noise that was more like a wretch than a cry was coming from deep inside and it was frightening.

238

"Why don't you go to my bed and lie there a minute? C'mon let me take you."

"Okay, Mommy." She sounded so little.

While tucking her under the covers, I said, "You know, you have talent."

"The agents won't be able to see it."

I could still feel her trembling. She said she was freezing. When I got the thermometer out, it shot to a hundred and two. Another unfulfilled dream of shining for Daddy had actually made her sick. I knew it was time for some special comfort. I asked her to close her eyes and try to relax while I placed my hand on her burning face. And just as she had done all those years ago when she was just a baby, Jen held onto my hand as I caressed her face and head. I sat there for a long time. When she was breathing easier and appeared to be cooler, I reached for the thermometer again. It registered temperature normal. She said, "Thank you, Mommy," and then fell deeply asleep. I tiptoed out of the room and quietly closed the door. She slept until morning.

The next day Jen's resilient spirit surfaced and a fresh outlook replaced the disappointment. She said, "It might even be better if Dad comes for graduation instead, which is good, but now I won't get an agent, which isn't."

I reminded her that most actors don't go to a special high school yet they have agents. She'd get one, too. She said she hoped so.

I was proud to watch my daughter perform her part with a professional dedication, and I thought she looked lovely on stage. But after the performances were over, she lost a little ground. "Mom, I don't want to go to school tomorrow."

"Why?"

"I won't get any calls from agents so, please, do I have to go?"

"You really were a wonderful dancing girl and I won't be surprised if you do get a call."

"That's ridiculous, Mom."

But the next morning she changed again and went to school just to see which of her friends had been noticed. No one was more surprised than she to find an agent's phone number posted under her name. Each morning the kids ran to the main hall to see the most recent name on the list. By the time it was all over, seven agents had left requests to see Jennifer.

She said, "Mom, I can't believe anyone noticed me in that part. Didn't I look fat?"

"Apparently seven agents didn't think so."

Both the senior play and graduation came and went without Dad. He wanted her to visit him that summer, but there were auditions with agents and a career to launch before taking off for California.

A flurry of activity began with audition appointments and decisions about which agent was best. I talked Jen into freelancing with the top three who offered representation. This would give us a better idea of which agent would do the best job of getting her career started. It made sense to find out firsthand. Jen agreed and told her three agents not to call until she got back from L.A. When she returned, I knew she had really grown up.

"Mom, you know how you always told me to speak to Dad about my feelings and about all the things he did that bothered me through the years? Well I finally got the nerve this summer."

"That's wonderful. How did it go?"

"Once I started talking everything, came out, and I even reminded him of that stupid thing about unhealthy attraction."

"That took courage."

"He was great and listened without saying a word until I finished and then said simply he'd made some mistakes. When he said he was sorry and that he loved me, all my anger was gone and I knew I'd completely forgiven him."

"Isn't it better to get things out in the open where they can be discussed? Jen, no parent ever wants to hurt their child and you gave yours a chance to let you know. That was a real gift you gave to Dad."

I knew one day this confrontation would take place but never dreamed it would happen at such a young age. I was really pleased that John had reacted so well. I had chosen him to be her father and had always wanted their relationship to be good. Jen had taken care of business and was ready to get on with her life.

Launching this career was exciting, exhilarating, and even exhausting. There were appointments to keep, decisions to make, and auditions to prepare. It brought back old memories when she asked me to help memorize the menu for her new job as waitress in a hamburger joint near our house. I enjoyed being part of it all and began seeing more of my daughter.

When winter came, it got to be less fun. Jen had auditions all over town and found that relying on public transportation wouldn't get her there on time. So I would drive her there myself, especially if it was to the lower west side where parking is next to impossible. I would wait for her outside in the car. When the temperature dropped to well below zero, it got pretty cold. If the appointment lasted as long as an hour, I was shivering with cold by the time she appeared. "I'm really sorry, Mom, but you can see we barely have time to make the next audition."

We'd tear off to the east side of Manhattan, discussing how well the last audition had gone, while she changed clothes in the seat next to me. I warmed my hands, one at a time, by sliding them under my thigh as I gave Jen the wisdom I'd learned years ago from many similar auditions. Jen always accepted my suggestions with open interest. Her desire and willingness to learn made me confident that she'd always do well.

My photography business was growing and there was always something to do or learn and on occasion, I even dated. But it was getting harder to deny that a cynicism toward men had crept into my view as I found myself refusing most offers for dates. I did want to share my interests with someone but I had to admit that I no longer felt much desire to be a partner. This was a sad situation for me because I really prefer to be with a man.

Jen received many positive reactions from auditioning and had screen tests for several new series. We went through the usual hell of waiting to hear if she got the part and the usual disappointment when she didn't.

When Jen failed to get one series in particular, it brought the issue of weight to a head. Convinced that she needed to take off a few pounds, she immediately sought help. For three months I stifled a gag as I watched her pour boiling water on small gray pieces of dry stuff, until they swelled into an unappetizing substitute for food. She said it's what the astronauts eat. I was sure there had to be an easier way. But she dropped the extra pounds in just a few months and this success brought a new confidence. She decided on her own that it was time to sign an exclusive contract with the most hard-working of the three agents.

After a year of auditioning and coming close without succeeding, unbeknownst to me, her next decision would force me to revisit a familiar pain. I feared that rejection might prove too discouraging, but instead of giving up, she planned a strategy that

I didn't want to hear. "Mom, I have to move to L.A. Everything is being cast on the West Coast and I'm just spinning my wheels in New York. Dad said I can stay with him until I find a place of my own." It was 1989, exactly one decade since my son had left home for college.

Every parent knows the day will come when the last child leaves home, but few are prepared for that day. To make life easier, I was outwardly supportive but I knew I would miss her desperately. I wept uncontrollably when alone. It took a while to make the arrangements. We had to tie up loose ends and pack a closet full of black clothes. Forcing my biggest suitcase to close was like wrestling an alligator. When the time came for the trip to the airport, I managed to be cheerful and tried to say only significant things. There was a lot to impart from this mother who was giving her last child to the world.

"Be careful driving and with boys. Get plenty of sleep. Eat healthy food. Go easy on my credit card. Call often and, oh, where's the *Vogue* magazine?" Yes, she had money for the movie and, no, she didn't forget anything.

"Mom, it's time for me to go." She looked very grownup as the attendant accepted her airline ticket, but when she turned to wave a final good-bye, she started to cry.

I was grateful that she walked quickly away and disappeared into the plane. Dropping into a nearby chair I let go of my feelings. *Please God, take care of my baby.*

When the aircraft rose effortlessly into a clear blue sky, I watched until it disappeared from view, then just stood there for a very long time, staring at nothing.

Jen, are you crying, too?

Chapter 18
RETURN TO L.A.

I TOOK MY TIME DRIVING back from the airport and hoped Jen would remember to call. When I opened the door and stepped inside, my house felt eerily empty. No one lived there any longer but me. I walked through the rooms with the ghosts of three other people and memories of times that were over. There were echoes of Johnny's infectious laugh, even John's, "What'd you do today?" and I could still smell Jen's scent in her room.

Johnny's things had long been removed and his room was bare except for my photography equipment in one corner, a small sleeper couch, a wall lined with books, and a desk near the window, where I spent hours working on my budget or pondering the meaning of life.

I went to the window and looked at the view where I'd

processed the news of Mother's death and barely two years later, John's wish to divorce. Now, after a decade or more, it was my first day of living here alone. The dinner table was much too symbolic, so I went to bed without eating. I tossed and turned all night. I knew that tomorrow would be better, but I allowed myself to grieve through the night.

By mid-morning the teachings of spiritual science began to kick in. I'd chosen this destiny for the growth it would bring and to sink into depression would not fulfill my part in the plan. As always, friends needed help with their problems and as soon as my phone started ringing, I gave my concern to their needs. It made me happy when they said I'd made a difference.

Jen did remember to call and was full of stories about life in California. "Johnny wants me to live with him but I have a room of my own at Dad's. And Mom, Dad said the most wonderful thing. He said I've grown into a lovely young woman and he's proud to be my father. I told him it was thanks to you because you took so much time teaching me."

"Darling, what a nice thing to say!" I hoped to myself that the boundaries between them would vanish. I truly wanted Jen to be close with her dad.

Jen kept me informed about meetings, auditions, and the progress taking place. Her New York agent had a branch office in Los Angeles and arranged to switch representation. He set up a meeting with the California team, who greeted Jennifer with aloofness bordering on disdain. It was her first bad experience with agents. "Mom, it really felt icky to sit in that conference room, surrounded by a circle of people who fired one question after another about my experience in film and weren't at all interested to hear about my work on the stage in New York."

246

"When they see how talented you are," I said, "their attitude will change and you'll learn a good lesson about show business. As soon as you sign a contract for a part on a series, the same people who didn't have time to be friendly will suddenly become your 'best friends.' Be nice to everyone but don't ever forget what I've said."

Just three months after Jen arrived in Los Angeles, she booked her first series, *Molloy*, to play the part of the stepsister to a young comic actress named Mayim Bialik. The girls worked well together and the show seemed destined for success. As if I'd had a crystal ball, those California agents were calling her darling and just couldn't do enough. Jen laughed when she said, "I see what you mean."

Johnny complained that he didn't see enough of his sister and she complained about his complaining. "Mom, I'm so busy and I barely have time for a telephone call." I guess that was a tip-off because right after that I, too, heard from her less. She was busy with work and getting settled. But New York is a long way from Los Angeles and I was waiting for that usual check-in call. It was a hard habit to break.

Jen suddenly decided to rent an apartment in one of the canyons, and I wished she had stayed at her dad's. She was safe at Dad's and I was pretty sure he'd keep an eye on things. She was barely twenty, overly generous, and earning a very high salary—a combination that easily attracts parasites. She made many new friends and although the women sounded nice, I wondered what the older guys had in common with such young girls. Jen felt I wasn't giving her credit for being an adult but I, like most parents, wanted to protect my child from potential harm.

Jen never did wake easily to an alarm and was arriving late for early morning studio calls. To solve the problem she asked me to please ring her telephone at five in the morning, saying, "It's already eight in New York and you're always up early." I became the reliable alarm clock and at the same time heard a rundown of the latest news. She found a car, the apartment needed furnishing, and I wanted to be there to help. My sister Joan and her husband said they'd do what they could. They hooked up the television I sent, showed her how to use the remote, then took her to dinner. A few days later, Molly invited her for dinner, too.

I was annoyed to find myself stewing about the years we'd been without her dad and hoping I'd done a good job of raising her myself. It hadn't been easy. I worried that maybe the problems of the divorce and the lack of money had made our life a bit dismal. Had I done enough to make up for the fragmented family? Does this second guessing go on in every empty nest?

How do other women manage alone after the last child leaves? Do they worry or feel lonely? It's funny about a mother's protective instincts; they don't leave with the child. Once again I began thinking about a support group. I wanted to share my doubts and related issues. These thoughts filled the empty space in my heart. There was too much time to think.

For me the expression "no man is an island" had more truth than merit. How profoundly the actions of others had affected my life. Everything had changed, many times, as a result of the departure or arrival of others. Most recently it had been my daughter's career move to the coast. I not only felt the ripple effects in my heart but also in my dwindling business. Many clients had come through Jen, and with her gone things really began to slow down.

To attract new business, I posted fliers around town. A few people responded. A friend pointed out the dangers of having strangers in the house, especially when only I knew they were there. But hiring an assistant was too costly. I was forced to take the risk.

I continued like that for a while but loneliness and fear took their toll. There was no longer a regular job to keep me in New York so I decided to have a long stay in California to surround myself with the warmth of family and old friends. I resurrected my old habit of saving pennies to buy a ticket. Fortunately an airfare war helped speed up the process.

Johnny was living with a roommate and Jen had too much company. I needed to find another place to stay. Molly invited me to be her guest and in just a few months I was packing to go.

Molly was jubilant as she greeted me at LAX. On the way to her house we talked about Johnny's career and his goal of becoming a motion picture director. I told her that although he had graduated from Loyola University with a degree in film, it was tough to break into any part of that business. He was struggling at the bottom in nonunion, lower-paying jobs that worked him sixteen hours a day. I couldn't understand why he agreed to do it, but he said, "I'll be a better director if I have experience in every aspect of the business. Each year graduates from film school flood the market, so if I don't, someone else will." I told Molly that lately he was being hired for better positions because he'd worked on that movie *Max and Me* last year. Molly said she remembered that Johnny had arranged for Jennifer to work as an extra. We agreed that it was typical of him to share his first break with his sister. He worked long, hard hours because he loved making movies. He approached the bad jobs with the same dedication and enthusiasm he gave to the good ones. I admired this trait.

We noted the dichotomy that one of my two talented children was struggling to over come hurdles, while the other was succeeding with relative ease, and that in both cases there was nothing I could do but sit by and feel helpless.

We were all surprised and disappointed when the Fox network canceled *Molloy*. But it wasn't long before NBC cast Jen in a new comedy series, *Ferris Beuller*. It was based on the hit movie and would costar Charlie Schlater, an actor we knew to be very talented. There was a strong chance it would be a hit. I was invited to visit the set and felt very proud. Everyone said I had good reason to be.

As the summer passed, I was slowly becoming acquainted with the people in Jennifer's life.

"Mom, there are so many new people I want you to meet as soon as we have time."

It had always made me happy that Jen liked my friends and I wanted to like hers, too. I had been looking forward to the time when our parent/child relationship evolved to the level of friends and that time seemed to be at hand. There was so much we could share as women. But old habits are hard to break and it was simply impossible for me to stifle my worries about her safety or hold back my stream of advice. I knew too much about dangers.

It was inevitable that my insights about show business and the managerial skills I'd developed long ago with her father would help Jenny's career get started and at the time she had been very receptive. But making her aware of the dangers that come with celebrity and money was quite another matter. My concern that others would take advantage of her conflicted with Jenny's trusting nature. I tended to sound old-fashioned and suspicious, as though I didn't trust her.

"Molly, she's too trusting."

"You wanted her to be trusting."

"But now I'm forced to point out it's dangers and I'm afraid it's causing trouble between us."

Molly told me not to worry. She did the same thing with her kids and they understood that it's natural for a mother to express her love through concern. Molly's words of wisdom always seemed to work wonders for me.

One night dinner with my sister Joan and her husband, Don, ended abruptly when they rushed me home with a migraine and an upset stomach. They pulled into the driveway and I flew out of the car just in time to throw up all over Molly's well-tended garden. What a mess. I was so embarrassed and terribly sorry. I saw Molly's love in action when she took care of the garden and me as if I were one of her children. She wouldn't allow me to feel bad or embarrassed. We had wonderful times in those seven weeks. Living together on a day-to-day basis gave us the chance to experience the true depth of our friendship. I'll always cherish those memories.

Then it was time to go home. Home?

I boarded the plane for my return to New York, hoping Jen understood my message but that I hadn't been too intrusive. I arrived home to a business that was slower than ever. When it hadn't improved by late fall, I put up more flyers.

A man called almost immediately; he seemed anxious to get new pictures and wanted to come over to see samples of my work. It was late in the afternoon and I wasn't busy, so I agreed when he said he couldn't arrive until eight. As soon as the line went dead, I was sorry for making an appointment in the evening and wished I had asked for a phone number.

At eight o'clock sharp the buzzer rang. I opened the door and was struck by his unusual height. There stood a man nearly as tall as the door, wrapped in heavy clothing to ward off the cold winter-like night. Off came the hat and gloves and in a couple of strides with those long lanky legs, he landed at the far end of the room. He was pulling off the scarf and making himself at home when I got an odd feeling. I hung back near the door and remained standing to discourage the jacket coming off. After unzipping half way, he got the message and remained standing too as he launched into a string of oddly formed thoughts. Then, without warning, he began talking about sex among the elderly and about two people he knew in particular who were well into their nineties and had frequent, wonderful oral sex with each other.

Okay, I'm no dummy. This is not a normal conversation and chances were that this guy wasn't normal either. So he was either here to repulse me to death or to demand oral sex before throwing my corpse off the terrace. I was alone in my apartment with a very tall guy who obviously hadn't come to look at pictures—and no one knew he was there. Damn, there was no record of his name or telephone number. If I ended up dead, he'd get away with murder. I needed to stay calm. Even if I could manage a scream, which I doubted, the walls in my building were soundproofed and no one would hear. I had to get him out of my house.

Backing toward the door, I spoke quickly, saying, "Do you ever get migraines? You know, I get them a lot. In fact one's coming on now and it's disturbing my ability to think. My husband is sick in the other room and my son's coming home any minute. I really don't do evening appointments. Can we reschedule?"

I flung open the door, stepped into the hall and, forcing a smile, held my breath. My blood ran cold as he walked past and said, "I'll call you tomorrow." I never heard from him again. My friends got testy. They said I'd had a very close call and should move the studio out of my apartment. Of course they were right, but with the high cost of rent in New York, it was my apartment or nowhere.

Soon it was winter.

Jen came home for the holidays, keeping her promise to never miss Christmas with me. My lack of business soon became obvious. I told her that except for a couple of her old high school friends who tried to connive a sitting for nothing, I'd had no calls at all. We discussed various options and I mentioned that I'd always wanted to write. I showed her a book, on loan from my friend, about basic writing technique and that the author suggests the best way to start is with your own autobiography. My friend thought I had had an interesting life and suggested I jot down some notes. Jen was very supportive and I agreed to keep her posted.

We made plans for a spectacular Christmas Eve dinner at Tavern on the Green and, to make the evening perfect, we invited Penelope. The days flew by and much too soon it was time to take Jen to the airport. I hated to see her go, and she promised to do better about calling. When I returned home, the house seemed emptier than ever.

In the weeks that followed I tried to begin writing, but I was surprised to find that traces of bitterness got in the way and made objectivity difficult. It was essential that I work further on emotional healing because negative feelings, lurking in my phrasing, were hurting no one but me. The notes were put away until later.

Jen's success was growing. I was proud, though worried, when personal managers looking for new clients began approaching her with offers all the time. It concerned me that so many more actors were hiring managers since the days when I worked in the business. In my experience, actors who couldn't get an agent or didn't have a star quality look would hire a manager to help in finding an agent or to improve their appearance. Jen had a hardworking agent and a natural, wholesome beauty. Hers was an image that appealed to a wide variety of people. I feared that a manager might interfere with what I saw as her strength and, as well, be a terrible waste of money.

Managers also have been known to expand their duties by taking control of a celebrity's personal affairs such as finances. I cautioned Jennifer that many successful actors had ended up broke after years of trusting their enormous earnings to the care of someone they hired and in some cases, had even grown to love them as part of the family. I felt Jennifer didn't need a manager and it was a big relief when her agent supported my position. So far, we'd been sufficiently convincing.

With my life going through another transition, it was easy to fall into worry and mounting depression. I had too much time to reflect and was beginning to buy into the widely held view that although it's admirable to be a full-time mother, it really doesn't prepare you to do anything else. By the time full-time mothering is over, it's hard to switch focus. There's also no retirement plan for mothers, and after thirty years as a mom, I needed another career. I tried to discover which avenue to take. But each new road pointed toward another dead end. Was I one of those displaced housepersons for whom a changing society hadn't yet found room? It took effort to stop feeling old and worthless.

When spring arrived, warm, sunny weather brought a lift to my spirits. Jen suggested that I move back to Los Angeles. Of course she was right, but I didn't know what to do with all that stuff.

Not long thereafter, Molly called with the shocking news that

254

she had been diagnosed with liver cancer. She asked if my knowledge of nutrition had revealed any new breakthroughs in alternative treatment. Molly's manner was casual, and it took a while for this terrible news to sink in. I told her I'd look into it. I mentioned that Jenny wanted me to move back to California. Molly started to cry and said she'd been praying I would. She hoped I'd come as soon as possible.

It took months to go through seventeen years of accumulated things, including what three others had left behind. The emotional strain was enormous. But by late October of 1991, the movers were packing what I hadn't discarded into a van and I was heading for California. After a lifetime of financial struggle and disappointment had diminished my capacity to want, it was a surprise to discover how very much I wanted to move back home.

Finding the right place to live took more time than I expected, but I finally chose an airy one-bedroom condominium, conveniently located between two freeways, that would do for the time being. My aesthetic sense was more than offended by wallpaper from the Fifties that covered most of the space, but Johnny came to my rescue. He and his friend Randy put in long days of back-breaking labor to remove every trace from the oversized rooms and then spent several more covering it all with a fresh coat of paint.

Getting settled and spending time with my ailing best friend were my two main concerns. Molly made it easy. Despite her deteriorating condition, she was cheerful and had a bright outlook. Although radiation had made her hair fall out, it was nearly impossible to tell she was sick. We laughed just as much at outrageous things. Even when her cancer spread to a brain tumor and interfered with nerve impulses to her limbs, our laughter brought us to tears as she described with great humor a time she'd lost control of one leg. Not since Mother had I seen anyone that brave. I felt sure my kindred friend would live forever.

One day when Molly's son phoned to say his mother had died a few hours before, I couldn't believe it. Molly dead? Impossible. We only had nine short months together! When she died, part of me died, too.

In my eulogy I told Molly's beloved family that on the day of her death, the earth had lost a bearer of kindness, but that the angels were singing with great joy and saying to each other, "Look who's come home."

I'll never get used to her absence.

In setting up a photography studio in Los Angeles, I was met with one obstacle after another. It was impossible to duplicate the available light I'd used in New York. I wasn't willing to restrict myself to studio lighting. Fearing the quality of my work would be less than I had delivered in the past, I decided to abandon photography as a business. The following year was spent processing the loss of Molly, looking for a car, and trying to find another kind of work. I was also feeling a bit out of place. Everything seemed to move slower in Los Angeles and I couldn't stop rushing at the fast pace of life in Manhattan. These were familiar surroundings yet not quite like home. Why hadn't I noticed during summer visits?

Johnny was usually tied up with a new girlfriend and I also saw too little of Jen. I joined the ranks of grumbling parents who don't see enough of their grown children. Once again I was wondering what to do next. I was determined not to feel defeated or old, but I realized it might not be easy to build a whole new circle of friends because the world isn't always friendly to aging single women.

I checked in with the local branch of my church and was struck by the minister's wisdom and helpful words. I signed up for a few sessions of counseling and was happy to discover that I'd already resolved some important issues. I was surprised to note a certain compassion for John had grown out of my gradual realization that he had missed the joy of watching our daughter grow into a woman. He would never share that warm feeling each morning when she appeared in the kitchen, half Jenny, half angel. By making a choice that had made her a guest in his house for much of her childhood, he deprived himself of experiences that sustain life well into old age. I was genuinely sympathetic.

With this understanding I knew I gained another level of freedom. Between the friends I made at church and regular meetings with a group doing spiritual study, I was forming a new life once again. An unexpected opportunity arose.

My hidden talent for drawing was discovered by my new friend, Bari, who wanted to expand her decorator business. Wrought-iron furniture was the latest craze, so she asked if I might try to design some pieces. It sounded exciting. After sketching a few examples, I received Bari's final approval on one of my designs and the go-ahead to get the line made. There were months of visits to the iron man's shop to watch my drawings become chairs or tables. I was pleased when the finished product received raves.

It turned out that the high cost of ironwork done locally made the profit margin too low and Bari had no choice but to discontinue production almost before it got started. It was a great disappointment for both of us. But at the same time I felt proud to have designed something that fine.

My third year in California was well under way and I was still wondering what to do with my life. Jen surprised me with a word processor for my birthday and the "writing" was on the wall. It took a while to overcome my resistance to the complicated technology but I knew it was time to try writing again.

When I finally sat down to begin typing, ideas arrived in rapid succession and the day seemed to end before it began. I believe this late bloomer had, at long last, discovered what it was she wanted to be when she grew up. At a point when it appeared I'd run out of options, the element of passion rushed in.

I was elated to discover, once again, *why* one must never give up.

Chapter 19
THE NEED TO "INDIVIDUALIZE"

T HE ANGEL OF CREATIVITY CAME to my house and touched everything with joy. I basked in wonder upon entering the fascinating world of imagination. A friend who wrote for television had given me pointers on structure and I was creating a sitcom for prime-time TV. Writing dialogue that turned characters into real people brought endless hours of pleasure. I could almost hear them speak out from the page to announce what they wanted to say. Sometimes I'd wake after midnight with an idea and rush to begin typing all night.

In the gentle climate of southern California a gift from my daughter ended a lifetime of longing when the destiny I'd been seeking found me.

The dreams Jennifer had fashioned at just eight years of age were coming true. I watched in amazement. Each day filled us all with quiet anticipation. I was reminded of those three happy years in the mid-Seventies when our family first moved to New York. I enjoyed being part of the process again. It was a wonderful time.

While working on location in Arizona, Johnny met Shannon, a girl he really cared about. When he returned she was left behind. Visits were too infrequent and when missing her became unbearable, a serious talk with Shannon's parents allowed her to move to Los Angeles. Jen and I were happy that Johnny had found someone we both liked so much.

When ratings fell short of what everyone expected, NBC canceled *Ferris Bueller*. Again we were disappointed. But it was only a matter of months before Jen was cast in *The Edge*, a comedy sketch review. The cast was very funny and the show was hilarious, but the ratings were not good. Success for yet another show seemed unlikely and it weighed heavily on her mind. Aware of the potential for harm in a business that devours its young for lunch and spits them out when the next meal is served, the watchful eye of Mom kept turning its gaze upon Jen.

Jen met Bari and some of my other new friends and liked them very much. She still wanted me to meet her friends. I was eagerly looking forward to that meeting, but work-related demands from Jen's busy schedule repeatedly interfered with our plans.

My greatest concern was Jen. Building an acting career creates a lot of stress and on occasion she called upon Mom's soothing hands. In response to the panic in her voice, I would rush over to give the comfort that always seemed to ease her pain. For emotional healing she turned to a different source. "Mom, I've consulted a therapist to work on boyfriend problems and some old issues with Dad."

260

Completely absorbed by my passion to write, another year flew by. It was late in 1993 and I was still engrossed in working on my sitcom. One day Jen said, "Mom, I've come a long way with that therapist and we wonder if you'd mind attending a few sessions." Her request came as a complete surprise. We had always communicated openly and well with each other, but if there was a need to do it in front a third party, I welcomed the opportunity to bring our relationship to an even higher level of understanding. One week later we met for the appointment in a beautiful house near the beach.

The therapist began with a long explanation about our children's need to "individualize," a word she used many times. I agreed with her wholeheartedly. Hadn't I helped mine begin that process years ago? The therapist ended her wordy introduction by reminding me that a person can't choose parents at birth but later, as adults, each of us can make choices about our parentage. I had read during spiritual study that human beings *do* choose their parents for very specific reasons but decided not to bring it up. I was eager to hear what my daughter wanted to say and glad when it was her turn to speak.

She spoke candidly. I listened with great interest and by the time she finished, we were both crying. I hugged her and said, "I'm sorry, Honey, it looks like I wasn't the mother you wanted me to be." It's true, I was no Donna Reed, but few of us are. "Darling, you've already told me, many times, that you didn't like me to yell or lose my temper when you misbehaved but preferred a more rational, conversational tone. But as I've told you before, it's a bad habit I learned from my dad and one I've nearly broken, though I certainly want to take this opportunity to apologize again." I also hoped for the chance, in this protected setting, to describe life as a single parent without the cooperation of Dad. Perhaps Jen would understand what it was like to raise a teenager in one of the world's most expensive cities with so little money, grappling with the changes of age. With mature objectivity, guided by this therapist, perhaps we'd both gain. We wiped our tears and I asked if it was my turn to speak.

Jen said, "Of course, go ahead, Mom."

But the therapist had other plans. I was interrupted and told about boundaries and informed that not only was my perspective irrelevant but that I was also trespassing some invisible line. When comments about "choices" were thrown into the mix, it seemed like I was being asked to prove myself worthy of being a mother or else. Wait and see, Nancy, this is too important, I thought to myself.

In the few sessions that followed, it was hard to avoid the realization that implicit in the concept "individualize" was the threat of a complete break. During each encounter, in one way or another, that threat was restated. I couldn't shake my negative gut reaction. If Jen needed to regain her power, why was she being pointed in the direction of me? Was being close to one's mother clinically regarded as pathology? Had mom-bashing found its home in the current psychoanalytic rhetoric? Was I merely to sit here like a target? How disappointing. My high hopes evaporated into thin air.

The stepfamily therapy had a bias against children and here was a view biased against the mother. There seems to be a supplier for everyone's need. On the long drive home to the valley, I wondered if this is what's happening to the American family.

During my next counseling session at church, I was trembling with fear at the thought of losing Jen. It was a loss I couldn't bear. Years ago I had made a deal with God to be a good person if He just wouldn't take my children. I confided to Reverend Jim, "I don't think I can make it without my daughter." The minister spoke seriously of the potential for harm in a joint therapy that puts demands on only one of the participants involved. He suggested I discontinue the sessions. How sad. Almost every grown person has misconceptions about their parents, as parents do about their children. But I simply didn't know how to convince her well-meaning therapist that the real threat to Jennifer was to be deprived of a mother who loved her more than anyone on earth. I hoped that one day Jen would realize that, although my flaws made her angry, my intentions had always been to provide whatever she needed in order to have the kind of life that was so elusive to me.

But if this therapist brought peace to Jenny's troubled mind when I couldn't, I had to be grateful.

Jenny and I needed to adjust to the changing dynamic between us. I gave some thought to a concept that wouldn't leave my mind. Was there something to this "individualizing" that I had overlooked? In my concern for Jen to find independence, had I neglected to see my own dependence on her? Since the day they were born I hadn't made a move without considering its affect on my children. But aren't mother's supposed to do that? I knew that those instincts had been strong in me even as a child but doesn't nature, or perhaps estrogen, give this protective tendency to all women? Of course. I decided to dismiss the idea as useless fodder for my already overworked tendency to worry.

I felt happy that my daughter was building her career before deciding to marry. It appeared that she would be spared many of the circumstances in which being a woman isn't always easy. She may have avoided a predicament in which masses of women are permanently stuck. Had she heeded my warnings or is this how destiny works? Perhaps a little of both.

Everyone concerned was fine with my decision to end the joint therapy. Jen was working hard and needed me less for guidance. With outside pressures threatening to break our ties, I hoped our lives wouldn't take off in two different directions. Confident that nothing could come between us, I put my doubts away. But they quickly returned when I finally got to know her friends. They were not my kind of people. I nearly swallowed my tongue, on more than one occasion, just to keep from saying, "Hey, watch your language." They'd whisper secrets in my presence and talk to each other as if I wasn't there. I felt awkward with such blatant, ill-mannered behavior and lack of human consideration. I'd always felt proud of Jen's gracious ways and the kindness she extended to everyone. This "hip" crowd showed little of that. Was I being too old fashioned?

I tried to adjust my expectations because hanging onto these people meant hanging onto Jen. But I wasn't a very good sport when they treated me like a visitor in my own daughter's house.

Johnny became engaged to Shannon and they planned to marry when she finished college. That old adage about a daughter giving you a son when she marries but losing a child when your son takes a wife was giving me a lot to consider. Was it true? Would his decision to marry create an emotional distance between us? I considered the possibility and cautioned myself that a cliché wouldn't prepare me for this one. I felt a little silly, so I decided to do us all a favor and put that one aside. She's a wonderful girl and will simply be one more person to love. Jen was also busy but kept in touch on the phone. I tried not to complain that I didn't see much of my kids. The old story.

I had been writing with great fervor for two years and had created a comedy show about a single mother who lives in New York with her two kids—a family similar to mine. I telephoned Jen to share my excitement with her. "I've finished writing my sitcom and am dying for you to read it. People are saying it's pretty good." She was the one person who truly understood how much it meant for me to find something that offered a promising future and was creatively fulfilling. I was surprised to learn how much I wanted her approval.

As both Jen and I suspected, *The Edge* was canceled but, again, Jen was soon cast in her fourth series, *Muddling Through*. The same concern arose about its future.

After some searching, Jen found a larger apartment, which helped lift her spirits. My telephone rang: "Mom, the movers are coming tomorrow and I don't know how to pack all this stuff!"

"Don't worry, Baby, I'll be right there."

"Mom, don't call me Baby."

"Sorry, Darling. Is Darling okay?"

"Mother!"

The new apartment was very nice and I was relieved to hear that going home after work meant that she would relax in the country atmosphere of the hills above Laurel Canyon and feel calmed by a spectacular view. I did find myself praying that she wouldn't be toppled by an earthquake or return home to the ravages of a fire.

One day NBC sent a script for a new sitcom that was expected to be the hit comedy of 1994. Jen said it was the best script she'd ever read and was very disappointed because being tied to another series on another network made it impossible to accept the offer. She found herself in a real dilemma. She desperately wanted the new series and I knew why after I read the script. I, too, believed it was going to be a big hit. Agonizing weeks followed as we waited to hear if the conflict between the networks had been settled.

It took time and some high-level negotiations but everyone worked out their differences in Jen's favor just in time for her to make the first day of shooting at Warner Brothers. It was one of the biggest hits of the season. I was delirious as millions of people fell in love with *Friends* and my daughter's fame grew. Her picture was in magazines all over the country and television shows lined up for interviews. It was the success we'd always imagined. Yet she ignored my advice and hired a manager. I couldn't understand why.

It wasn't long before Jen signed with a new agent and a whole staff was rounded up to take charge of her every need. A business manager, a publicity man, a lawyer, a personal assistant, and she told me that even a maid was found by the manager. Ironclad contracts had been signed and a coterie of strangers had taken over her life. My fears had been realized. Through the years I had grown used to Jennifer turning to me for advice on important decisions and now it was painful to find that I had been replaced. It was too brutal. Too fast.

I went to church for more counseling. The minister suggested that because of the years we had been alone together, my influence may have been too strong and this might be a necessary step for Jen in finding her own destiny. Whatever the reason, I knew it was her life and if she needed to make independent choices, I hoped the stakes weren't too high. Life offers us many lessons and by now it was obvious that Jen's would be quite the opposite of mine.

266

It was also time to concede that I had nothing in common with Jennifer's friends, and they had even less in common with me. I reached a point where I could no longer tolerate their rude behavior or dismiss it as a difference in age. When my innocent gestures were misrepresented to Jen, I began to suspect that my presence was somehow threatening. I began to feel myself being eased out of the way.

Most parents know it's a mistake to admit having concerns about their grown children's friends, so I hid my feelings. As Jen's fame grew, the constant stroking was hard to watch. I always hoped that one day Jen would have a friend like my Molly, but for now there seemed little hope of that. It was sad to watch, so I initiated a policy of having our visits at the studio on the set of *Friends*. We weren't able to talk privately very much, but at least we were in an atmosphere of respect and kindness and I could leave with a good feeling. It made me happy to find that her new friends made their high regard for Jen obvious by the considerate way they treated me.

The tide of fame had rolled in, bringing with it the flotsam and jetsam of Jennifer's destiny. Despite our differences, these were exciting times for our family. Aunts, uncles, cousins, and friends were having fun in the magic of Jen's celebrity. How I wished that Molly had been there. Johnny felt a brotherly pride for the little sister he so deeply adored. When he set a date to marry Shannon, we were all ecstatic. Jen and I stood with them at the altar, giving our blessings, as the happy couple exchanged vows about forever.

I had given my sitcom to Johnny to read and a top writer's agent said it was good, but I was still anxious for Jen's approval. She was excited and fully occupied with the recent purchase of a beautiful house in the Hollywood Hills. Her usual dilemma arose: "Mom, help. The movers are coming the day after tomorrow and I haven't had time to pack. I'm stressing big time."

"Don't worry, I'll be there in the morning."

It was an especially hot day and I was glad that a couple of her friends had stopped by to help. But when I tried to move a cardboard wardrobe I had just filled with Jen's clothes, neither one of them lifted a finger to help as they watched me struggle to move the heavy box out of the way. I wondered why they were there.

Jen hired an interior decorator and filled her house with gorgeous antiques. I was pleased to see how very much alike we still are in taste. When Johnny and his new wife returned from their honeymoon in Greece, Jen gave them a lavish reception in her stunning new home. Family members and friends of many years came to meet my new daughter.

My fragmented family, at last, had a chance to grow into the traditional one I'd always wanted. We were building bonds of love with our newest member and counting our many blessings.

Chapter 20
NEW INSIGHTS

WHO COULD HAVE KNOWN ON Johnny's wedding day that just six short months later the treachery of a tabloid TV show would put an end to my joy? When the emotional ties that form strong bonds of trust in relationships were weakened, our family split apart.

There's an ancient Greek tale about the goddess Demeter who loses her daughter to another world. The story foretells the agony of any mother who looses a child. In the two-and-a-half years that followed, I felt Demeter's pain many times. The miracle is that I've survived the broken bonds of my precious mother/daughter relationship and in the overcoming became stronger and more free.

What rocked me to the core turned out to be the vehicle that led to a process of healing and peace I wouldn't have found in any other way. For a person who spent the last twenty-five years in spiritual study, I was amazed that there was so much work to do on my inner self and that the change could be so profound. It's as if another person inhabits my being, a person quite unlike the one who began life as a daughter, then the girl who married in her teens, or later, the woman who twice became an ex-wife and a single mother. In my search for answers, each role that defined me was set aside along the way. Something deep within changed. The pain of believing that I may have lost my daughter forever helped me to redefine myself as Nancy the "human being" who can best serve all relationships, including a future one with Jen.

The process of solitary introspection and subsequent entries in my journal lifted the curtain of despair as it led me to re-evaluate perceptions about the past. New insights were changing the way I had been looking at things.

During the first year of separation from Jen there wasn't much in me but pain. I went on day after day writing in my journal, sustained by the progress being made. I took regular breaks to experience more fully the gains. Long walks and discussions with a few friends helped illuminate the way as new bonds of friendship grew between us. I was becoming part of a community of people who express goodness in deeds. Each one seemed to say that fulfillment comes from seeking truth and they all showed unusual respect for human striving. The support from these people was the element I had longed for in the traditional family that simply wasn't destined to be.

One day a tiny angel arrived who would soon call me grandmother. With her arrival God placed divine grace in my life. It was unfathomable joy to watch Johnny hold his baby. To see that big burly guy gently caressing an infant in two muscular arms warmed my heart every time. When she cried, he spoke in a most tender way. It was deeply moving to watch my grown child caring for his own tiny daughter. Love worked its magic on me. My son was now a parent and I hoped he had the understanding and patience to keep his family unit strong. I thought of the troubled young woman who had left his father, all those years ago, and felt quite selfish. I hoped for the sake of that baby that the example of my divorce hadn't become a life principle for him.

For a long time most of my friends didn't know that there was no contact between me and Jen. But her growing fame made hiding the truth more and more difficult. Well-meaning friends or acquaintances often asked how it feels to have a famous daughter. It feels great of course, but it's hard to speak while holding back tears. To the most frequently asked question I always respond, "No, I don't see her very often. She's terribly busy." Coloring the truth about our separation is against my principles but I feel much too ashamed to tell.

I became less ardent about keeping the separation secret when Penelope gave me a bestselling book about daughters who give their moms a hard time. During years as a therapist, the writer of this book had found that estrangement from grown children is epidemic in our society. She describes the terrible pain and shame borne by the abandoned parents and tells of their rather elaborate methods to hide the truth. She writes that guilt and shame are universal. I wasn't alone in my feelings and apparently most other parents also find this truth too shameful to tell. I hope one day to give up the need.

When doubt plays its discordant tune and nags me into feeling guilty, the author's ground-breaking view that a daughter must accept responsibility for part of the problem helps ease the agony of self-incrimination.

I've come a long way in the three years since my journey began. By now you could wrap fish in the news that I *was* too dependent on Jen and needed a separation as much as she. I've also come to understand that life in that traditional family would have made it impossible to ever give birth to my own individuality. A dependent nature such as mine would have been completely absorbed by unconditional love and would never have known that moment when I felt the extraordinary awakening of me as a being—someone distinct from any roles that defined me in the past. While I believe there is merit in devoting one's life to other people's problems, I now understand that it takes a well-developed sense of self to know what someone else needs and that such a sense of self had eluded me.

John had said, "Your dreams didn't come true, Nancy." I now know that I wasn't dreaming suitable dreams. My focus had centered on transitory things and not on the unchangeable qualities in the human soul, life-sustaining qualities that form from the substance of loss and pain.

I can also see that the people who have hurt me the most in life are the ones who deprived me of my dreams—dreams that would not have been right for me. Odd as it may sound, those folks have my most sincere gratitude. Their actions forced me to build the strength to accept and understand that my daughter no longer required mothering; what she really needs me to be is her friend. Not knowing that, I might have been doomed to finish my days in the lonely shell of a stubborn, critical, bitter, old woman. I abandoned the idea of God as a dispenser of reward and punishment because it was clear that adversity had always been attracted by a part of me that needed the lesson.

One important issue remained unresolved. I was still finding it difficult to bring order to the chaos of my irreconcilable ideas about Jen. Doubts about some of her professional choices and my disagreement with the decision to have her presented in a more sultry image continued to bring conflict within me. After mentally dissecting the dynamics involved, another revelation liberated me.

When my babies were in the womb, it felt as if they were part of my own body. A few years after Johnny's birth this feeling gradually began to subside. I was quite startled to find that, all these years later, I was still experiencing Jennifer as me. It was beginning to make sense. If Jen is essentially me, she ought to benefit from all that I've learned, so I felt it was my job to teach her everything. It was inevitable that as she approached her mid-twenties we began to disagree about almost everything. I now see that our disparate views were trying to tell me that I hadn't accepted the fact that we are two different people with different lessons to learn. It had also been impossible for me to find harmony with publicity pictures that seemed to compromise her wholesome image until I accepted that our needs and values aren't the same. We're alike in many ways, but in that career move the view reflected is so counter to mine that a casual observer might think she had been raised by someone else. How could Jen have turned out otherwise? I had always encouraged my children to express their uniqueness. Yet when confronted with the dissimilarity that such expression demonstrates, I resisted. Once again light was cast on the shadow of misunderstanding.

But would these factors prevent a reconciliation? Will we ever be able to bridge the gap that separates our thinking? In counseling sessions with Reverend Jim, we pondered those questions. He encouraged me to believe that I am entitled to preserve my ideal attitude and conduct of living because they live in the root of my character. The strength I have deep within comes from integrity, unshaken by the storms of life. At the same time, Jennifer's views must be given equal consideration—the same consideration one gives to a friend. He added that unconditional love will help us to accept our differences. There's no guarantee at this point, but I know that I must be true to what I believe or I am useless to everyone, including myself.

As I shifted my thinking in this way, I knew I needn't worry about Jen anymore. My newfound confidence in her choices brought a sense of relief and freedom. I can now actually see that she's a grown woman. The taste of freedom is sweet.

Occasionally I experience discomfort when I attend meetings of an organization I belong to whose members work in the media and have chosen to unite their efforts to help restore morality in the entertainment business. I have found myself listening as someone singles out *Friends* as another show that shouldn't be aired during family time hours because young viewers are adversely affected by the bad language and the portrayal of sex as recreational. I sit in my anonymity feeling torn apart inside, one part of me agreeing with their sentiments and the other wanting to defend the daughter I love. I knew that the creative people involved with the show preferred a later time slot but that those decisions were made by people whose main concern is audience demand.

Only the passage of time will show if our mutual pain has given Jen and me the strength and understanding to bridge our differences. It was a big step for me to fully understand that I am not required to agree with everything that belongs to her life, "a place I can't go, not even in my dreams."

Recognizing that the past lives in the present and inhibits the ability to process events without bias was making me freer to live in the moment, less influenced by the spin of unseen forces. I can't give a clinical explanation of just why the process of keeping a journal helped me survive devastating loss and come out the other end more intact than ever before. I do know that something happens when you recreate an event so fully that you relive the experience and the feelings, painful or happy, as if they were happening for the first time. I found that the process must be done alone because the presence of another person, no matter how skilled, can influence the memory, causing a biased view or indulgence of pain. While held captive in the solitude of writing, memories unfold free of judgment. They speak with a voice I haven't heard, and of things I need to know. With each return to an event new insights emerge. The last time I reviewed the pages of my life, I shed fewer tears.

It is one magnificent miracle that I'm approaching the possibility of real freedom and the radiant presence of lasting peace. Fulfillment has come in many ways. A close relationship with Johnny, who gave me a special daughter-in-law to love, who in turn gifted me with a most glorious baby granddaughter, is a constant source of unimaginable joy. They have a wonderful family and each morning my prayers are sent to bless their union.

Years of working his way up from the bottom really paid off for Johnny. He learned so much about making movies and working with actors that he's now an excellent assistant director. When I hear news of each success, it fills me with pride. He's a successful, married man with a child of his own, but to me he'll always be the little blond boy who wanted to help take care of his new baby sister. The wonderful thing about having children is that the love streaming effortlessly to them from your heart can serve as an unending source of happiness if it is consciously directed to others. In return, friendship is infinitely more satis-fying. I need only think of my dear Molly.

In the third year of our separation, Jen and I made an attempt to reconcile. We spent a wonderful day just talking and catching up on things. Jen spoke of working on a short film with her brother. "Mom, Johnny's the best A.D. I've ever worked with." I was delighted to know that she recognized her brother's talent and that their relationship continued to be strong. But after one happy day together our relationship didn't improve, and once again con-tact between Jennifer and me ceased. I had waited for my mother to come back until the end of her life; if necessary I will wait until the end of mine for Jen.

For the purpose of allowing both parent and child to "indi-vidualize," it may be necessary for parents to separate from their grown children. (This need seems to hit mothers and daughters the hardest.) But if everyone involved continues to hope that it's a temporary thing, it may lessen that devastating feeling of living with death every day.

For now my life is in recovery and I feel positive about the future. Pain has propelled me to new ways of thinking and my feelings still rush to keep up. A wise old woman once said that separation can be good because, if there had been a healthy foun-dation, something wonderful can arise in the space that's left.

This isn't the end for Jen and me. Just a pause that allows "something wonderful" to arise in a space that's free of our mutual demands and expectations. I know that, for now, without me it will be easier for her to become the unique human being we all want to know. God willing, there's still so much more for us to share as women when we can transform our relationship from mother and daughter to friends.

276

No one can control the future, but I now can choose to control my reactions. I've made a silent promise never to "suffer" loss again. When people or things leave my life or enter at any given moment, I will strive to view it as a need for change, change that is a necessary part of existence, orchestrated by higher wisdom for everyone's good.

Few days pass when I don't miss Jen. Her fame brings constant reminders. If it becomes too overwhelming, I sink into a comfortable chair and remember twenty-six years of blessings brought by her presence. My newborn baby; my delightful, fascinating toddler; my wide-eyed little girl; my cranky teenager; and that stunning young woman discovering the world. My Jen.

More than three years have now passed since the day we first separated, and the feeling of loss is just as intense, as if it happened yesterday. Until Jennifer and I reconcile, I suspect it won't go away. When I first lost contact with her, there was nothing inside of me but misery. I have recently noticed that my pain has been gradually dwarfed by the richness I now allow to enter my life.

I have been privileged to feel enormous love for my children and that's their eternal gift to me. This love is always there softly glowing inside of me, and only causes pain when I diminish it with expectations. Once the barriers were down I discovered an appreciation for the smallest things. There were so many wonderful people to love. Life for me has become infinitely enriched.

The rogue tabloid media will get its due in the end. I can still hear their assurances that the viewing audience would find my comments about the Waldorf school's curriculum interesting. The director's parting words, "You'll call to thank me when you see how good you were," echo in my mind from time to time. And that attractive young woman who asked the questions had gained my confidence by talking about the wonderful man she married, then hugged and kissed me good-bye. In thinking back, I'm convinced they were laughing at me all the time. They must have known about the actors' boycott of their show and felt they had really put one over on one "stupid" mom. But my anger is gone—I've had the last word.

On the night of that angry telephone call from Jen, the world became a strange, unhappy place. For a long time my life was reduced to irrelevance as I wandered through the dark, searching for a concept, a thought, anything to hang onto. I had no way of knowing then that a wonderful journey in self-discovery was about to begin.

Thank you, Jen.

It is not the critic who counts. Not the man who points out how the strong man stumbled or where the doer of deeds could have done better. The credit belongs to the man who is actually in the arena. Whose face is marred by dust and sweat and blood. Who strives valiantly, who errs and comes up short again and again.

Theodore Roosevelt